Guitar Chords 101

Over 800 Common Chords, Plus Helpful Music Theory Sections

by Michael P. Wolfsohn

CONTENTS

ISBN 978-1-5400-6185-0

Visit Hal Leonard Online at
www.halleonard.com

Contact Us:
Hal Leonard
7777 West Bluemound Road
Milwaukee, WI 53213
Email: info@halleonard.com

In Europe, contact:
Hal Leonard Europe Limited
42 Wigmore Street
Marylebone, London, W1U 2RN
Email: info@halleonardeurope.com

In Australia, contact:
Hal Leonard Australia Pty. Ltd.
4 Lentara Court
Cheltenham, Victoria, 3192 Australia
Email: info@halleonard.com.au

About This Book

This book has been designed to be more than just a catalog of chords. It is intended as a multi-function harmonic reference source for guitarists.

The key to its usefulness is its organization. It is organized around each chord's root note and harmonic function rather than around root notes alone. This allows it to work in three ways:

- as a chord dictionary
    - when you encounter an unfamiliar chord in a song that you want to play you can look it up here, just as you would look up an unfamiliar word in a language dictionary.

- as a chord substitution guide
    - when you are trying to decide what kind of chord to use in a progression (or are looking for a "better-sounding" chord to substitute for the one that's already there) you can look for one here. In addition, there is a reference section that explains how chord substitutions work, and which chords may be substituted for other chords.

- as a harmonic reference
    - when you are looking for the next chord that would commonly occur in a chord progression (whether you wish to use it or to avoid it) you can look it up here. There are also several sections that explain chord progressions and other important considerations in music theory.

This book will be a powerful tool and an important aid to your musical development.

Half Steps and Whole Steps

The chords in this book are grouped by harmonic function: the role they play in standard chord progressions. In order to get the most use out of this book, an understanding of harmonic functions is important, and this will require some understanding of music theory.

While basic music theory topics will be covered in this book, you can gain a more thorough understanding of theory by consulting one of the many excellent books or courses that deal with music theory exclusively and in depth, such as *Hal Leonard Guitar Music Theory*.

In the meantime, this book will explain basic music theory, from basic definitions to more complex ideas including harmonic functions.

The basic building block of Western music is the half step. A half step is the distance between any given note and the next nearest possible note. On the guitar, this is a distance of one fret.

A whole step is the same distance as two consecutive half steps; on the guitar this is a distance of two frets.

Here are some examples of half steps and whole steps.

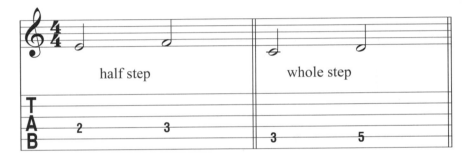

It is important to note that the distance between the notes stays the same (and the interval sounds the same) no matter where the notes are played on the guitar. The distance between this particular C and D, for example, is always a whole step whether they are both played on the same string or not.

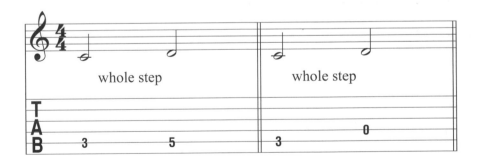

Major Scales

Now that you understand the basic difference between half steps and whole steps, you are ready to learn about major scales. A major scale is a sequence of eight notes that meets the following criteria:

1. It proceeds through all the notes in letter name order, with none skipped or repeated. This also means that on a standard notation staff, a major scale proceeds through consecutive lines and spaces with none skipped or repeated.

2. The first note and the last note have the same letter name. The last note is an octave higher than the first.

3. It may contain sharps or flats, but not both.

4. It proceeds through the following sequence of half and whole steps:

    Whole–whole–half–whole–whole–whole–half

Every major scale meets these requirements. Here, for example, is a C major scale with the half and whole steps shown.

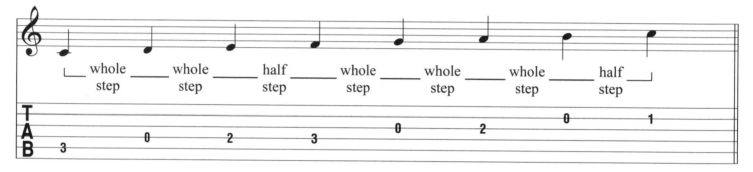

Sharps and flats are added to make the scale conform to the required sequence of half and whole steps. This table shows which sharps and flats must be added to make major scales beginning on any of the twelve notes. The sharps and flats in each key are listed in the order they appear when added to the standard notation staff.

Key	Sharps/Flats
C	(none)
D♭ (C♯)	B♭, E♭, A♭, D♭, G♭
D	F♯, C♯
E♭ (D♯)	B♭, E♭, A♭
E	F♯, C♯, G♯, D♯
F	B♭
F♯ (G♭)	F♯, C♯, G♯, D♯, A♯, E♯
G	F♯
A♭ (G♯)	B♭, E♭, A♭, D♭
A	F♯, C♯, G♯
B♭ (A♯)	B♭, E♭
B	F♯, C♯, G♯, D♯, A♯

The next step toward understanding harmonic functions is to understand intervals. An interval is the distance between two notes, as measured on the staff.

Each interval has two names: a general name (second, third, etc.) which refers to the number of note names the two notes are apart from each other, and a specific name (major, minor, etc.) which refers to the color of the interval. Intervals belong to one of two families: the major/minor family or the perfect family.

The following abbreviations will be used throughout this book when referring to intervals:

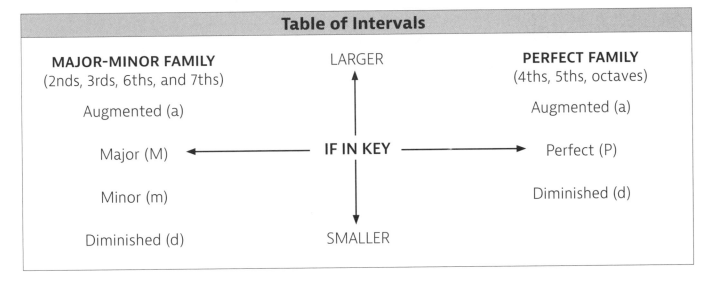

Table of Intervals

MAJOR-MINOR FAMILY (2nds, 3rds, 6ths, and 7ths)	LARGER	**PERFECT FAMILY** (4ths, 5ths, octaves)
Augmented (a)	↑	Augmented (a)
Major (M)	← IF IN KEY →	Perfect (P)
Minor (m)		Diminished (d)
Diminished (d)	↓ SMALLER	

To identify an interval, first find its general name by counting the number of letter names between the two notes, including the lines or spaces on which both notes are sitting.

Then find the specific name by doing the following:

1. Find the major scale that begins on the lower of the two notes. If the upper note is in that scale, then the interval is major (if it belongs to the major/minor family) or perfect (if it belongs to the perfect family).

2. If the upper note is not in the scale, determine how many half steps closer together or farther apart the two notes are than they would be if the upper note were in the scale. Then move up or down the chart that number of half steps to find the specific name of the interval.

Here are a few examples of intervals with their names.

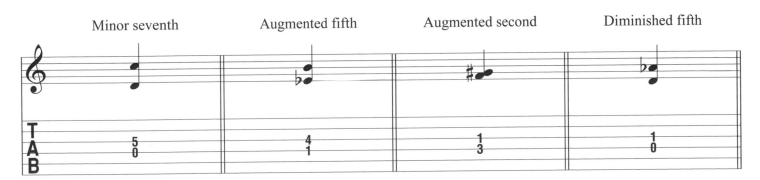

Minor seventh   Augmented fifth   Augmented second   Diminished fifth

Triads and Sevenths

Triads and sevenths are the two types of chords used in describing harmonic functions.

A triad is a three-note chord with the notes in specific intervallic relationships. The lowest of the three notes is called the root, or name tone. The interval from the root to the middle note will always be some type of third, and the interval from the root to the upper note will always be some type of fifth.

Notice that all the intervals are named from the root. This is also true when you build larger chords, such as sevenths.

A seventh is a four-note chord that contains a third and a fifth (just like a triad) plus some type of seventh (between the root and the octave).

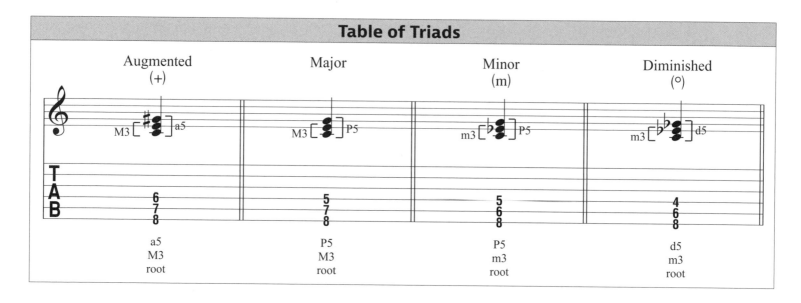

The triads built on the steps of a major scale are called diatonic triads. These are all the triads possible in a major key. Any other triad will be out of key.

To construct diatonic triads, begin by writing out a major scale. Then build triads on each note of the scale, using only the three notes in that scale, and no others.

Starting on C, you would get these triads:

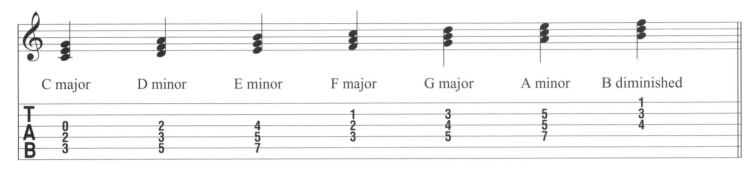

This sequence of triads (major–minor–minor–major–major–minor–diminished) is referred to as the diatonic triads for a given major key.

Diatonic triads are commonly referred to by the scale degree of their roots. In Roman numerals this would be as follows:

I–ii–iii–IV–V–vi–vii°–I

Numerals in upper case refer to major chords, numerals in lower case refer to minor chords. The single oddity is the diminished chord built on the seventh degree of the scale.

Diatonic seventh chords may be constructed in the same way. The only one that concerns us right now is the one built on the fifth (or dominant) scale degree. This seventh chord, which consists of a major third, a perfect fifth, and a minor seventh (also called a flat seventh and often thought of as being a minor third away from the fifth), is called a dominant-type seventh. It is customary to refer to these chords simply as "sevenths."

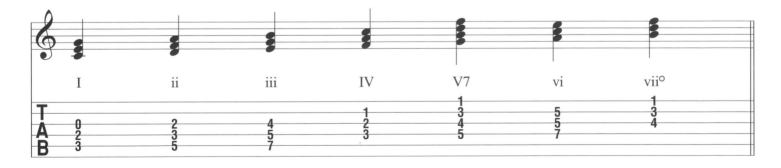

Harmonic Functions

There are only three roles that a chord can play within a major key. It can function as a major chord, a minor chord, or a dominant seventh chord.

Let's look at what each of these chords does within a major key.

Major chords serve as anchors in the key.

They help to define it as a major key. The most important major chord in a major key is, of course, the one built on the name tone for that key. Thus, in the key of C major, the C major chord is the tonic or I chord. Music in major keys tends to end on the I chord. In fact, a piece of music in the key of C could be thought of as being basically a series of chords designed to lead around to a final C chord at the end. Major chords can also be found on the fourth and fifth degrees of the scale. These are considered the pillar chords of the key. Every note in the scale can be harmonized by one of these major chords.

Minor chords add color to the key.

While every note in a major key can be harmonized by one of the three major chords in the key, music written with nothing but major chords can become dull. Minor chords help relieve this dullness by adding a different color (or sound quality) to music. Minor chords also help progressions along because of their tendency to move to the chord (within the key) built on the note that's found four scale steps above their own roots. For example, in the key of C, D minor tends to move to G7; E minor tends to move to A minor; and A minor tends to move to D minor.

Dominant seventh chords define the key.

Dominant seventh chords are unique in several ways. First, while there are two major chords and three minor chords in any key, the dominant seventh chord can only be built naturally in one place: on the fifth (or dominant) degree of the scale. Second, while both major and minor chords are consonant (they can stand on their own), the dominant seventh is dissonant (it traditionally must resolve to another chord, in this case the tonic or I chord). The need for the dominant (or V7) chord to resolve to the tonic is so strong that this progression alone can define a key. That is, when you hear a G7 chord move to a C major chord, it is generally safe to assume that you are in the key of C major. The seventh chord built on the fifth scale degree of the major scale is called the "dominant" because it "dominates" the key. It can single-handedly define the key. NOTE: Diminished and augmented triads often function as dominant chords, even without inclusion of a flat seventh.

Chord Substitutions and Alterations

Since there are only three harmonic functions, all other chords can be thought of as substitutes for, or chromatic alterations of, one of the three.

Substitute chords are usually employed to "disguise" or "soften" the effect of a major, minor, or (especially) seventh chord. For example, the ninth chord (which is a seventh chord with a major ninth interval added to make a five-note chord) functions just like a seventh chord but is not as harsh-sounding.

Play these two V–I progressions in C major.

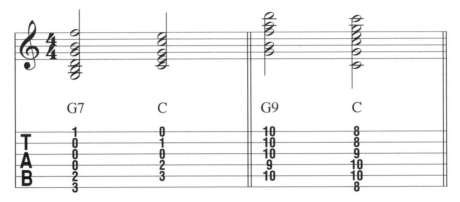

Notice that while both the G7 and G9 chords are dissonant and want to resolve to C major, the ninth chord in the second progression is less dissonant, or softer, and sounds like it has less of a need to resolve. Similarly, other chords can be substituted for any of the three main types of chords to change their effect (without changing their function).

Chords can also be chromatically altered. The most common alterations are the raising or lowering (sharping or flatting) of the fifth or ninth degree in chords that function as either minors or sevenths. This is usually done for one of two reasons:

1. If a note in the melody of a song is one of these notes, the chord is frequently altered to match the melody.

2. A chord may be altered to create a particular melodic motion or bass line. For example, the chord progression C–Am–Dm–G may be altered as follows in order to create a melody that descends by half steps:

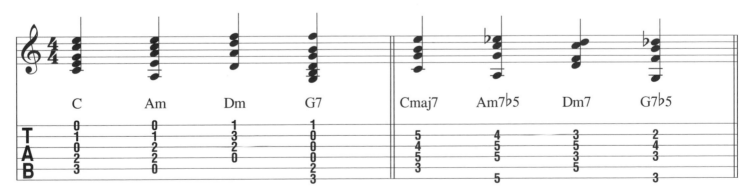

Chord Construction

Just as triads are constructed of three notes in specific intervallic relationships, so other chords are constructed of specific intervals. On these two pages you will find tables showing the intervallic construction of 36 commonly used chords (tables for triads and seventh chords are on pages 18, 19, and 20).

While tablature is given for each chord in this section to show you where the notes are on the guitar, not all of these root position chord forms can actually be played on the guitar. None of the seven-note chords, for example, can be played as written because the guitar has only six strings. Some of the five- and six-note chords would require five or six left-hand fingers to play as written.

Therefore, the guitar tablature on these two pages is for reference only.

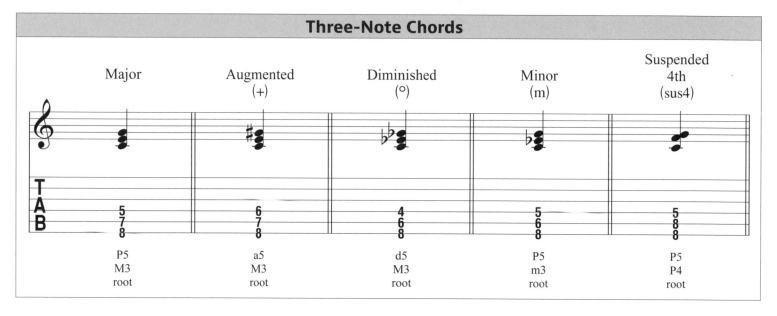

Four-Note Chords

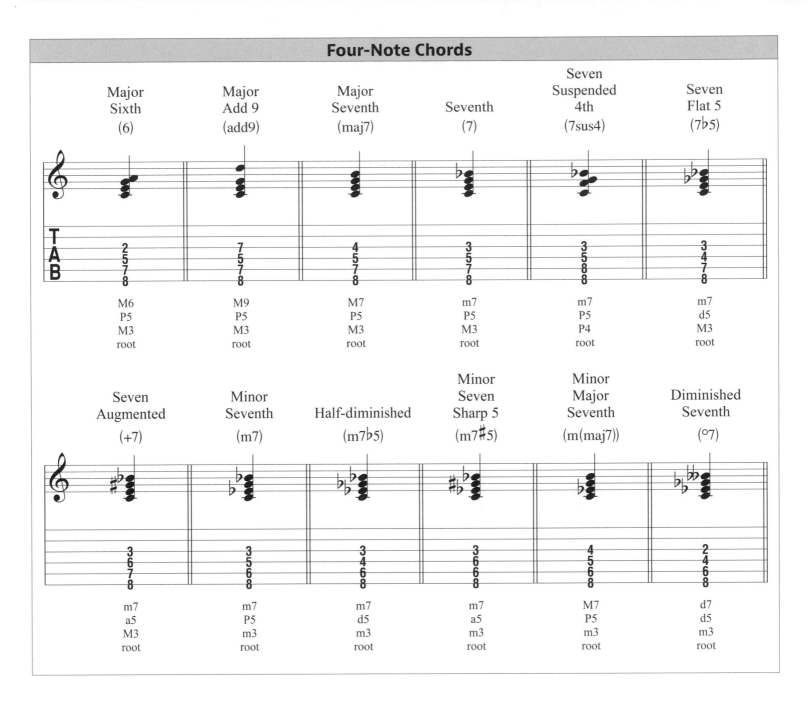

Chord Construction

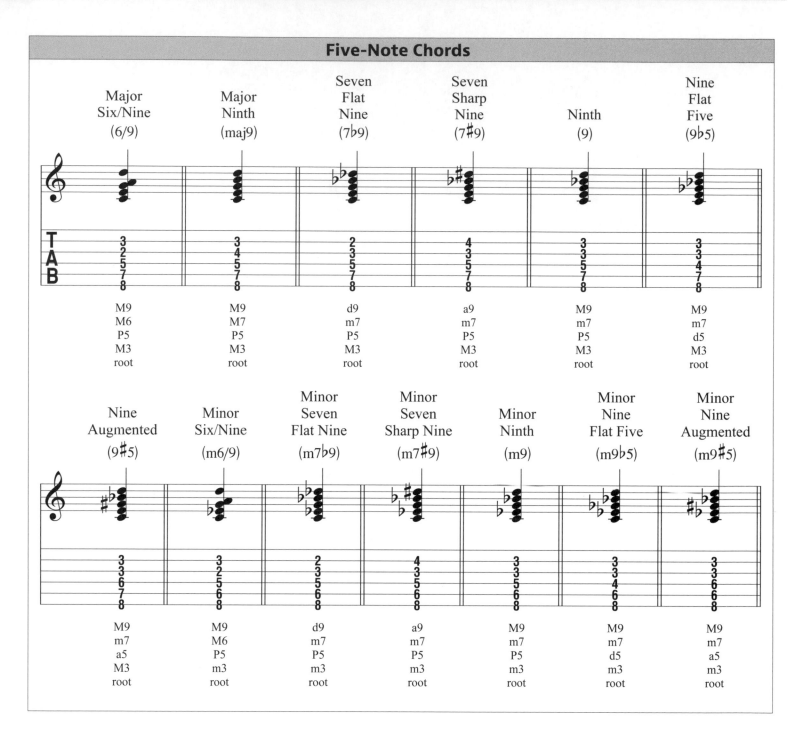

Five-Note Chords

Major Six/Nine (6/9) — M9, M6, P5, M3, root — TAB: 3 2 5 7 8

Major Ninth (maj9) — M9, M7, P5, M3, root — TAB: 3 4 5 7 8

Seven Flat Nine (7♭9) — d9, m7, P5, M3, root — TAB: 2 3 5 7 8

Seven Sharp Nine (7♯9) — a9, m7, P5, M3, root — TAB: 4 3 5 7 8

Ninth (9) — M9, m7, P5, M3, root — TAB: 3 3 5 7 8

Nine Flat Five (9♭5) — M9, m7, d5, M3, root — TAB: 3 3 4 7 8

Nine Augmented (9♯5) — M9, m7, a5, M3, root — TAB: 3 3 6 7 8

Minor Six/Nine (m6/9) — M9, M6, P5, m3, root — TAB: 3 2 5 6 8

Minor Seven Flat Nine (m7♭9) — d9, m7, P5, m3, root — TAB: 2 3 5 6 8

Minor Seven Sharp Nine (m7♯9) — a9, m7, P5, m3, root — TAB: 4 3 5 6 8

Minor Ninth (m9) — M9, m7, P5, m3, root — TAB: 3 3 5 6 8

Minor Nine Flat Five (m9♭5) — M9, m7, d5, m3, root — TAB: 3 3 4 6 8

Minor Nine Augmented (m9♯5) — M9, m7, a5, m3, root — TAB: 3 3 6 6 8

Six-Note Chords

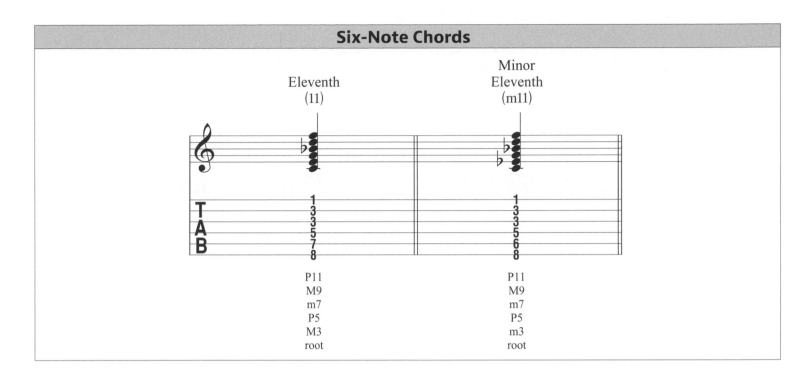

Seven-Note Chords

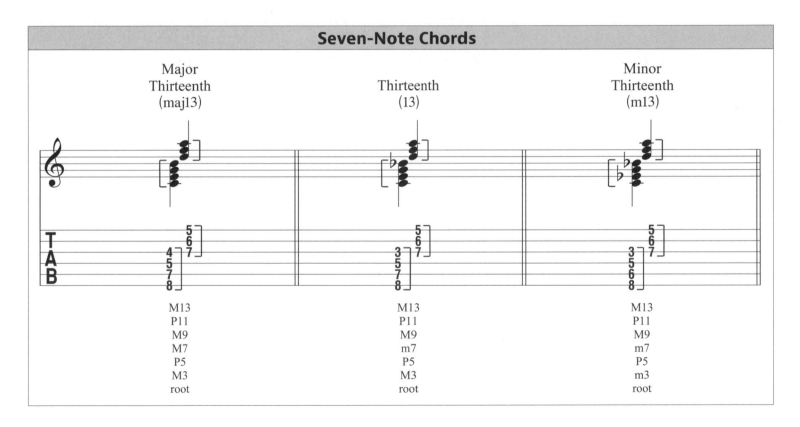

Necessary Notes in Chords

Not every note in a chord is necessary for its color and harmonic function to be heard clearly. For a guitarist dealing with the limitations of a fretboard, this is a very useful fact. The following table tells you which notes make up the full spelling of a chord, and which of these notes are absolutely required to create each chord type. Notice that the fifth scale degree is most commonly omitted (9 or 11 may also be left out if that scale degree does not directly name the chord—when playing with an ensemble, a guitarist may even exclude the root of a complex chord in favor of the chord's more colorful notes!).

Major Chords					
Chord	**Notes in Chord**	**Required Notes**	**Chord**	**Notes in Chord**	**Required Notes**
Major	R, 3, 5	R, 3, 5	maj7	R, 3, 5, 7	R, 3, 7
sus4	R, 4, 5	R, 4, 5	6/9	R, 3, 5, 6, 9	R, 3, 6, 9
6	R, 3, 5, 6	R, 3, 6	9	R, 3, 5, 7, 9	R, 3, 7, 9
add9	R, 3, 5, 9	R, 3, 9	maj13	R, 3, 5, 7, 9, 13	R, 3, 7, 13

Minor Chords			Dominant Seventh Chords		
Chord	**Notes in Chord**	**Required Notes**	**Chord**	**Notes in Chord**	**Required Notes**
Minor	R, ♭3, 5	R, ♭3, 5	°	R, ♭3, ♭5	R, ♭3, ♭5
m6	R, ♭3, 5, 6	R, ♭3, 6	+	R, 3, ♯5	R, 3, ♯5
m7	R, ♭3, 5, ♭7	R, ♭3, ♭7	7	R, 3, 5, ♭7	R, 3, ♭7
m7♭5	R, ♭3, ♭5, ♭7	R, ♭3, ♭5, ♭7	7sus4	R, 4, 5, ♭7	R, 4, ♭7
m7♯5	R, ♭3, ♯5, ♭7	R, ♭3, ♯5, ♭7	7♭5	R, 3, ♭5, ♭7	R, 3, ♭5, ♭7
m(maj7)	R, ♭3, 5, 7	R, ♭3, 7	7♯5	R, 3, ♯5, ♭7	R, 3, ♯5, ♭7
m6/9	R, ♭3, 5, 6, 9	R, ♭3, 6, 9	°7	R, ♭3, ♭5, °7	R, ♭3, ♭5, °7
m7♭9	R, ♭3, 5, ♭7, ♭9	R, ♭3, ♭7, ♭9	7♭9	R, 3, 5, ♭7, ♭9	R, 3, ♭7, ♭9
m7♯9	R, ♭3, 5, ♭7, ♯9	R, ♭3, ♭7, ♯9	7♯9	R, 3, 5, ♭7, ♯9	R, 3, ♭7, ♯9
m9	R, ♭3, 5, ♭7, 9	R, ♭3, ♭7, 9	9	R, 3, 5, ♭7, 9	R, 3, ♭7, 9
m9♭5	R, ♭3, ♭5, ♭7, 9	R, ♭3, ♭5, ♭7, 9	9♭5	R, 3, ♭5, ♭7, 9	R, 3, ♭5, ♭7, 9
m9♯5	R, ♭3, ♯5, ♭7, 9	R, ♭3, ♯5, ♭7, 9	9♯5	R, 3, ♯5, ♭7, 9	R, 3, ♯5, ♭7, 9
m11	R, ♭3, 5, ♭7, 9, 11	R, ♭3, ♭7, 11	11	R, 3, 5, ♭7, 9, 11	R, 3, ♭7, 11
m13	R, ♭3, 5, ♭7, 9, 11, 13	R, ♭3, ♭7, 13	13	R, 3, 5, ♭7, 9, 11, 13	R, 3, ♭7, 13

Table of Chord Substitutions

This table tells you which of the three harmonic functions these 36 chords serve. It can also tell you which of the 33 altered chords are always, usually, or rarely acceptable substitutes for the three original chord types.

Function	Always	Usually	Seldom
Major	Major Sixth	Major Seventh	Major Ninth
	Major Six/Nine	Major Thirteenth	
	Major add 9	Suspended Fourth	
Minor	Minor Seventh	Minor Sixth	Minor Seven ♭5
	Minor Ninth	Minor Six/Nine	Minor Seven ♭5 / Minor Seven ♯5
		Minor Eleventh	Minor Seven ♭9 / Minor Seven ♯5
		Minor Thirteenth	Minor Nine ♭5 / Minor Nine ♯5
Seventh	Seventh Suspended Fourth	Seven ♭5	
	Ninth	Seven ♯5	
	Eleventh	Seven ♭9*	
	Thirteenth	Seven ♯9	
	Augmented	Nine ♭5	
	Diminished*	Nine ♯5	
	Diminished Seventh*		

* The diminished and diminished seventh chords must be built on the note one half step above the root of the seventh chord that they are replacing. They function as a seven ♭9 chord with no root and with the ♭9 in the bass.

Major Triads (Strings 1-4)

The table on this page gives you three movable forms of major triads on strings 1–4 and tells you which triad you are playing at each position from open to 12th fret. Above the 12th fret, the table repeats—simply subtract 12 from the fret number to find the triad on this table.

These triads are all in closed position, meaning each successively higher note is the next possible chord tone. Since triads consist of three notes and these forms consist of four, you may play strings 1–3, strings 2–4, or strings 1–4, and still play the complete triad.

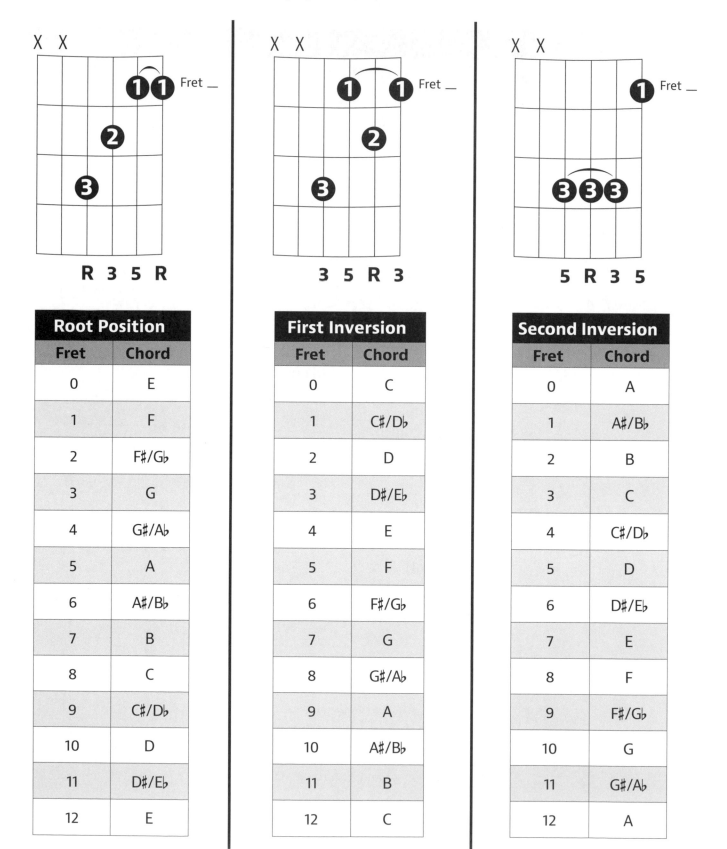

R 3 5 R   **3 5 R 3**   **5 R 3 5**

Root Position		First Inversion		Second Inversion	
Fret	Chord	Fret	Chord	Fret	Chord
0	E	0	C	0	A
1	F	1	C#/Db	1	A#/Bb
2	F#/Gb	2	D	2	B
3	G	3	D#/Eb	3	C
4	G#/Ab	4	E	4	C#/Db
5	A	5	F	5	D
6	A#/Bb	6	F#/Gb	6	D#/Eb
7	B	7	G	7	E
8	C	8	G#/Ab	8	F
9	C#/Db	9	A	9	F#/Gb
10	D	10	A#/Bb	10	G
11	D#/Eb	11	B	11	G#/Ab
12	E	12	C	12	A

Minor Triads (Strings 1-4)

This table gives you three movable forms for minor triads on strings 1–4.

These triads are also in closed position. They are very similar to the major triads found on the previous page, except that here the third degree of each triad is lowered one half step to form the minor chord. Again, you may combine strings 1–3, strings 2–4, or strings 1–4, and still play all the notes of the complete triad.

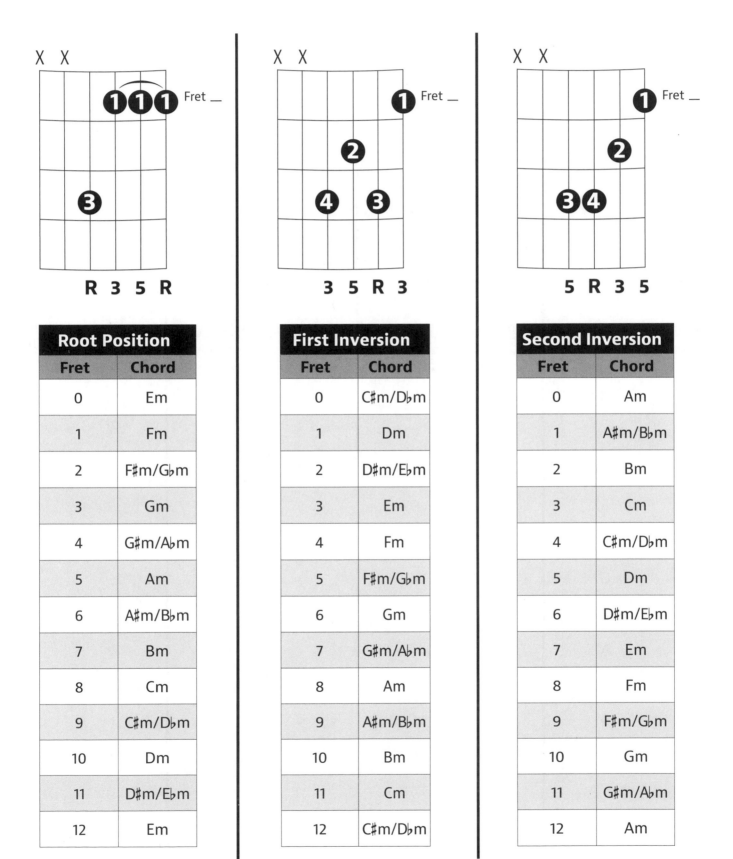

Root Position	
Fret	Chord
0	Em
1	Fm
2	F#m/G♭m
3	Gm
4	G#m/A♭m
5	Am
6	A#m/B♭m
7	Bm
8	Cm
9	C#m/D♭m
10	Dm
11	D#m/E♭m
12	Em

First Inversion	
Fret	Chord
0	C#m/D♭m
1	Dm
2	D#m/E♭m
3	Em
4	Fm
5	F#m/G♭m
6	Gm
7	G#m/A♭m
8	Am
9	A#m/B♭m
10	Bm
11	Cm
12	C#m/D♭m

Second Inversion	
Fret	Chord
0	Am
1	A#m/B♭m
2	Bm
3	Cm
4	C#m/D♭m
5	Dm
6	D#m/E♭m
7	Em
8	Fm
9	F#m/G♭m
10	Gm
11	G#m/A♭m
12	Am

Sevenths (Strings 1-4)

Small seventh chords work a little differently on the guitar than triads do.

Since there are four notes in a seventh chord, there are four possible inversions. Also, because there are four notes, you must play all four strings to complete the seventh chord.

Closed position sevenths are very awkward on the guitar, and therefore, are not very useful. The forms in these tables are the ones that are most commonly used.

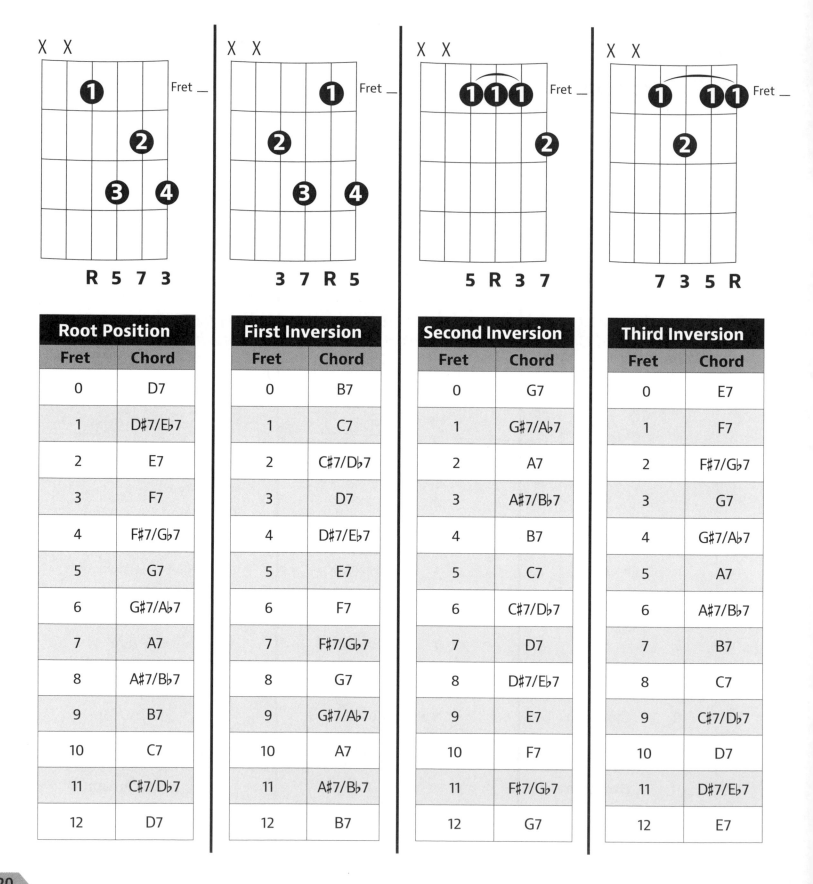

R 5 7 3   3 7 R 5   5 R 3 7   7 3 5 R

Root Position		First Inversion		Second Inversion		Third Inversion	
Fret	Chord	Fret	Chord	Fret	Chord	Fret	Chord
0	D7	0	B7	0	G7	0	E7
1	D#7/Eb7	1	C7	1	G#7/Ab7	1	F7
2	E7	2	C#7/Db7	2	A7	2	F#7/Gb7
3	F7	3	D7	3	A#7/Bb7	3	G7
4	F#7/Gb7	4	D#7/Eb7	4	B7	4	G#7/Ab7
5	G7	5	E7	5	C7	5	A7
6	G#7/Ab7	6	F7	6	C#7/Db7	6	A#7/Bb7
7	A7	7	F#7/Gb7	7	D7	7	B7
8	A#7/Bb7	8	G7	8	D#7/Eb7	8	C7
9	B7	9	G#7/Ab7	9	E7	9	C#7/Db7
10	C7	10	A7	10	F7	10	D7
11	C#7/Db7	11	A#7/Bb7	11	F#7/Gb7	11	D#7/Eb7
12	D7	12	B7	12	G7	12	E7

It is not feasible to include every form of every chord in existence in one book—there are just too many possibilities. Choices must be made in assembling any chord book.

In this book I have used the following criteria in selecting chords and chord forms for inclusion:

1. I have included all the basic first position chords that beginners are likely to need.

2. I have included all the most commonly used substitute and altered chords for each harmonic function.

3. I have included only chords in root position, except for the 7♭9 chord type which has the ♭9th as the lowest note. Inversions throughout can be derived without too much difficulty.

4. I have tried as much as possible to include one chord form with its root on the sixth string, one with its root on the fifth string, and one with its root on the fourth string for each chord. It was not always possible to do this.

5. Where there are more than three movable forms for a chord type, I have tried to use all of them at one time or another. Thus, if you are looking for a particular chord (say G♯ major seventh), you might try looking at the same chord type (in this case, the major sevenths) in other keys too; you'll just have to move the chord up or down the neck to bring them into the desired key.

There are more chords listed in the previous tables than are diagrammed in the following chord frames. You can always use the tables that cover chord construction along with the "necessary note" table to try to construct forms other than the ones given. And remember, when playing in an ensemble, it's perfectly fine to play just a few choice notes from a chord, especially if the other foundational notes of the chord are being played by the other instruments.

You can also have notes other than the root on the bottom of the chord. This will alter the harmonic effect somewhat. No matter how far apart the notes are, what sequence they are in, or how many times they are repeated, as long as at least one of each necessary note is present, the chord retains its harmonic function; and it is always acceptable to omit a repeated scale degree within a chord, unless the style of music requires it.

There are many other chord forms possible. If you don't find it here, that doesn't mean that it doesn't exist. A greater understanding of music theory and a good working knowledge of the fingerboard will help you to decipher whatever strange chords you may encounter—and even let you discover your own!

C Major

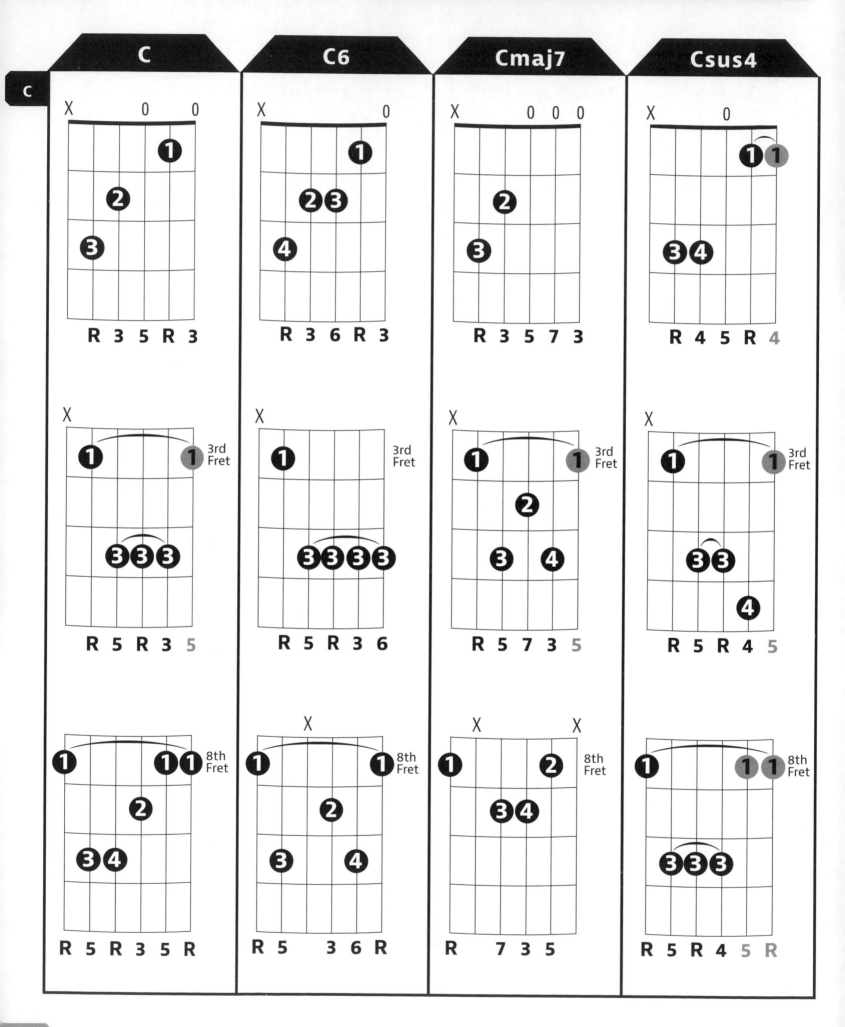

Minor   C

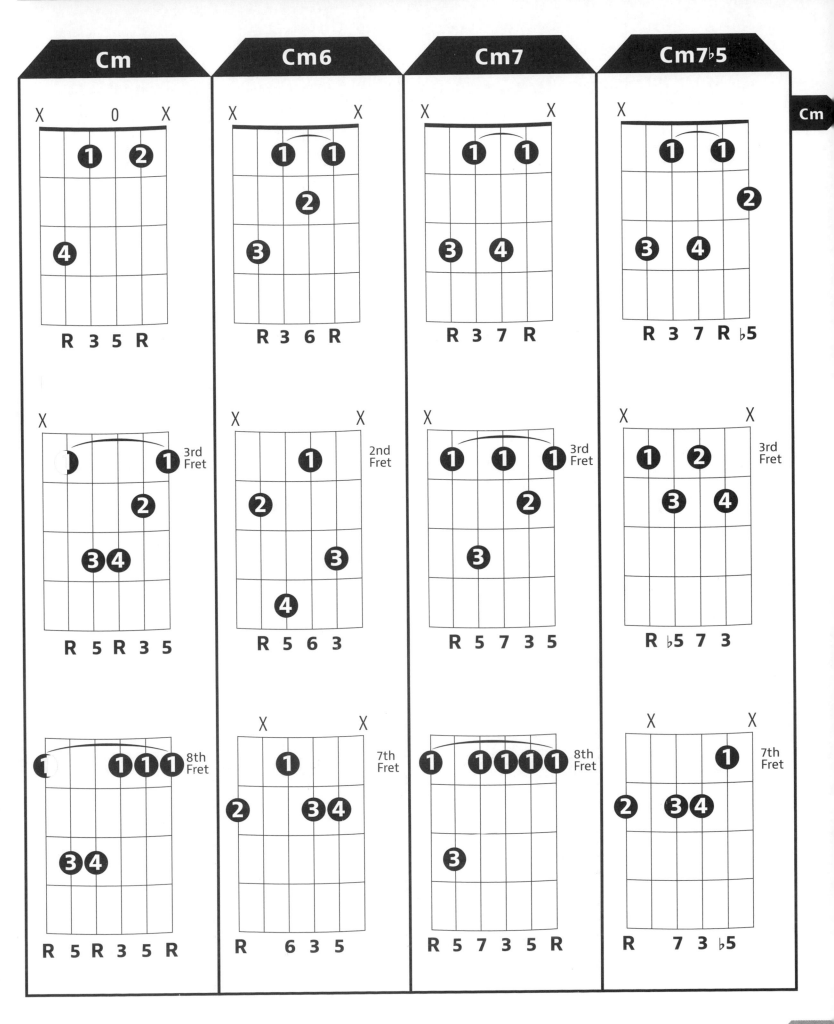

Cm

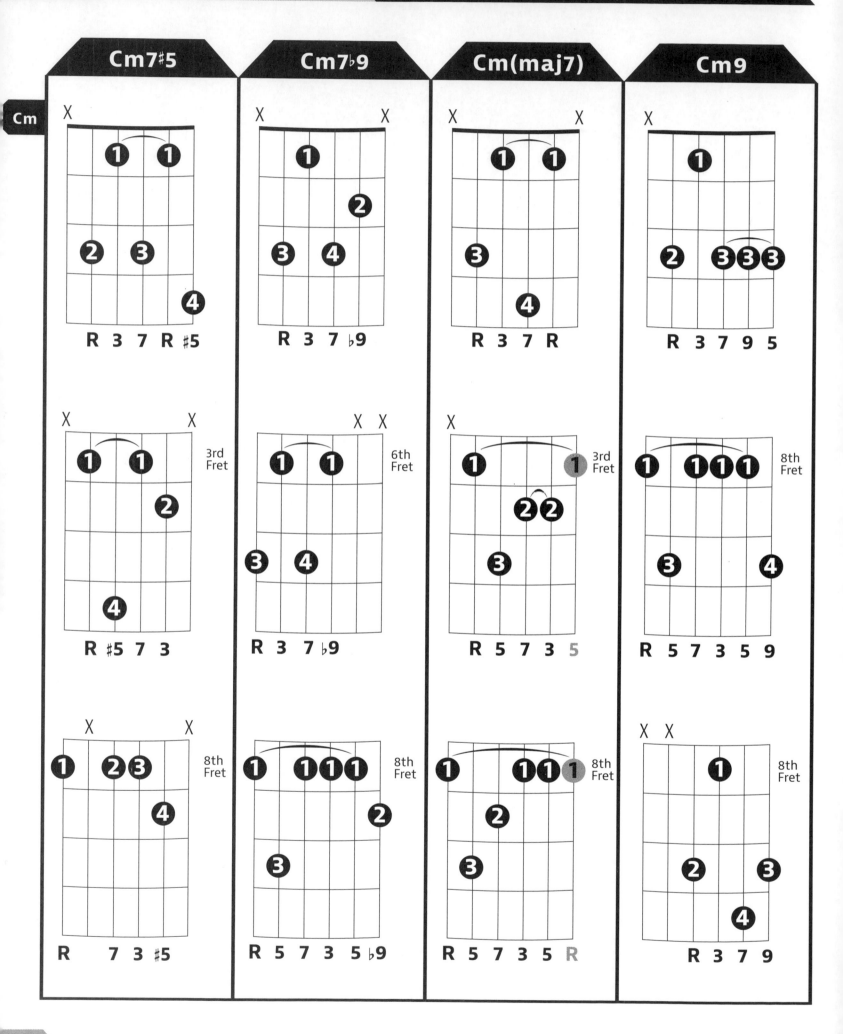

Cm7#5

R 3 7 R #5

R #5 7 3

R   7 3 #5

Cm7♭9

R 3 7 ♭9

R 3 7 ♭9

R 5 7 3 5 ♭9

Cm(maj7)

R 3 7 R

R 5 7 3 5

R 5 7 3 5 R

Cm9

R 3 7 9 5

R 5 7 3 5 9

R 3 7 9

Seventh

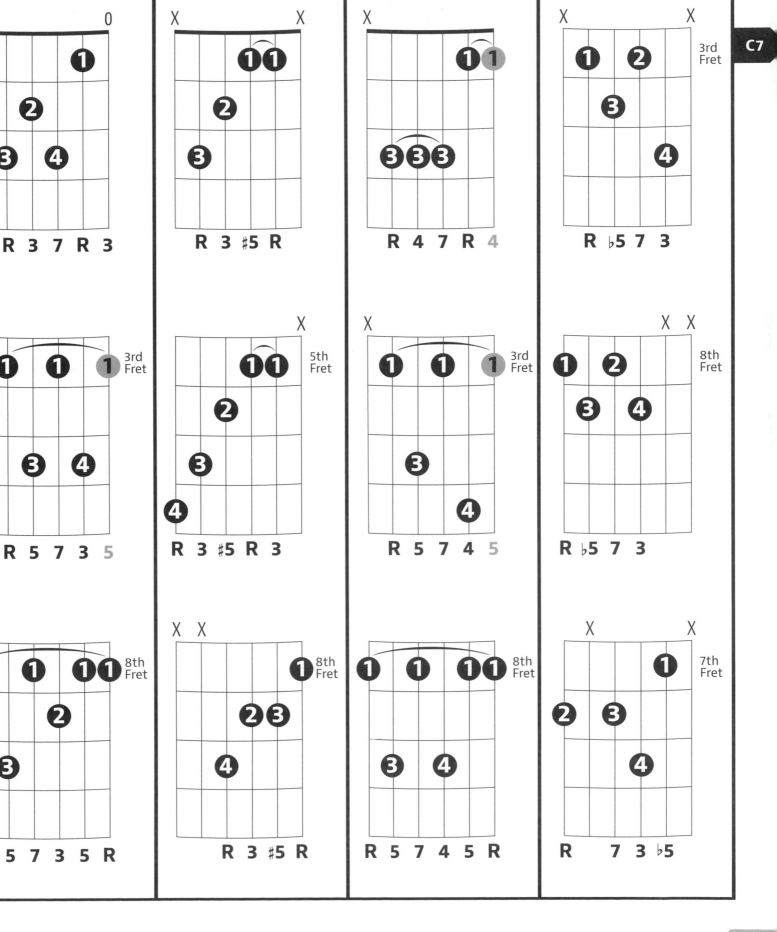

C7

C+

C7sus4

C7♭5

C   Seventh

C7

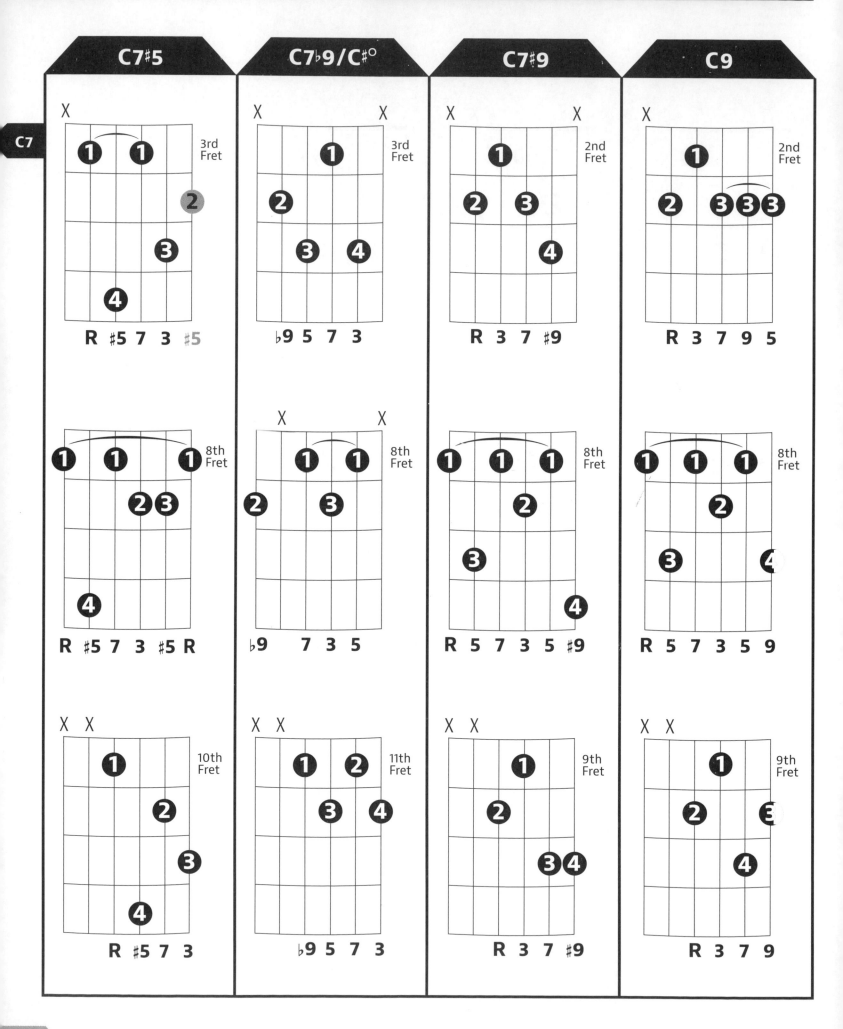

C7#5

R   #5   7   3   #5

R   #5   7   3   #5   R

R   #5   7   3

C7♭9/C#°

♭9   5   7   3

♭9   7   3   5

♭9   5   7   3

C7#9

R   3   7   #9

R   5   7   3   5   #9

R   3   7   #9

C9

R   3   7   9   5

R   5   7   3   5   9

R   3   7   9

3rd Fret   3rd Fret   2nd Fret   2nd Fret

8th Fret   8th Fret   8th Fret   8th Fret

10th Fret   11th Fret   9th Fret   9th Fret

26

Seventh   C

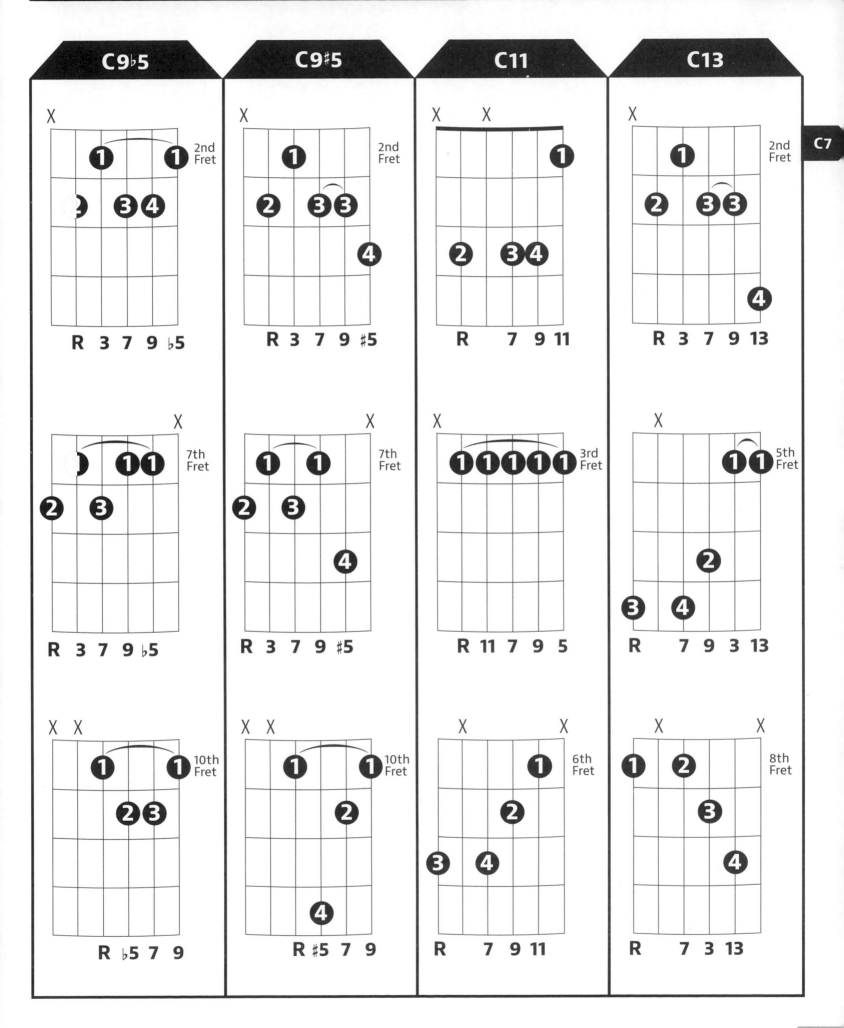

C9♭5

X

2nd Fret

R 3 7 9 ♭5

C9♯5

X

2nd Fret

R 3 7 9 ♯5

C11

X   X

R   7 9 11

C13

X

2nd Fret

R 3 7 9 13

X

7th Fret

R 3 7 9 ♭5

X

7th Fret

R 3 7 9 ♯5

X

3rd Fret

R 11 7 9 5

X

5th Fret

R   7 9 3 13

X   X

10th Fret

R ♭5 7 9

X   X

10th Fret

R ♯5 7 9

X   X

6th Fret

R   7 9 11

X   X

8th Fret

R   7 3 13

D♭/C♯   Major

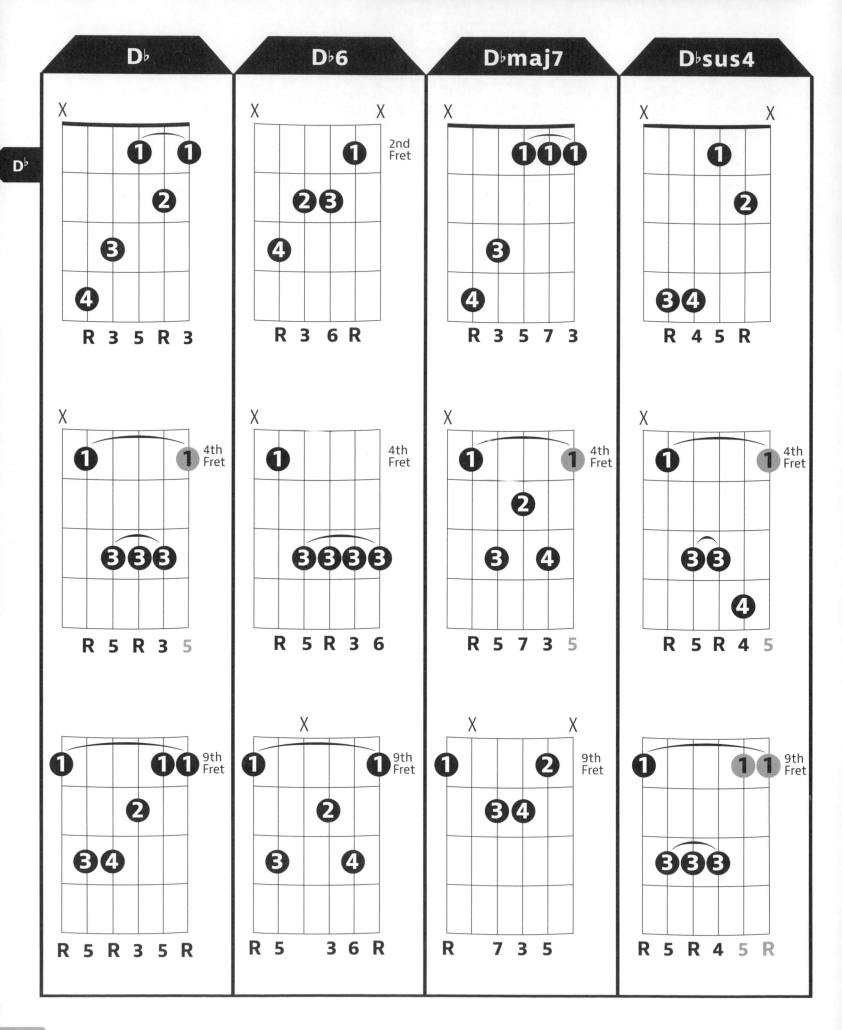

Minor

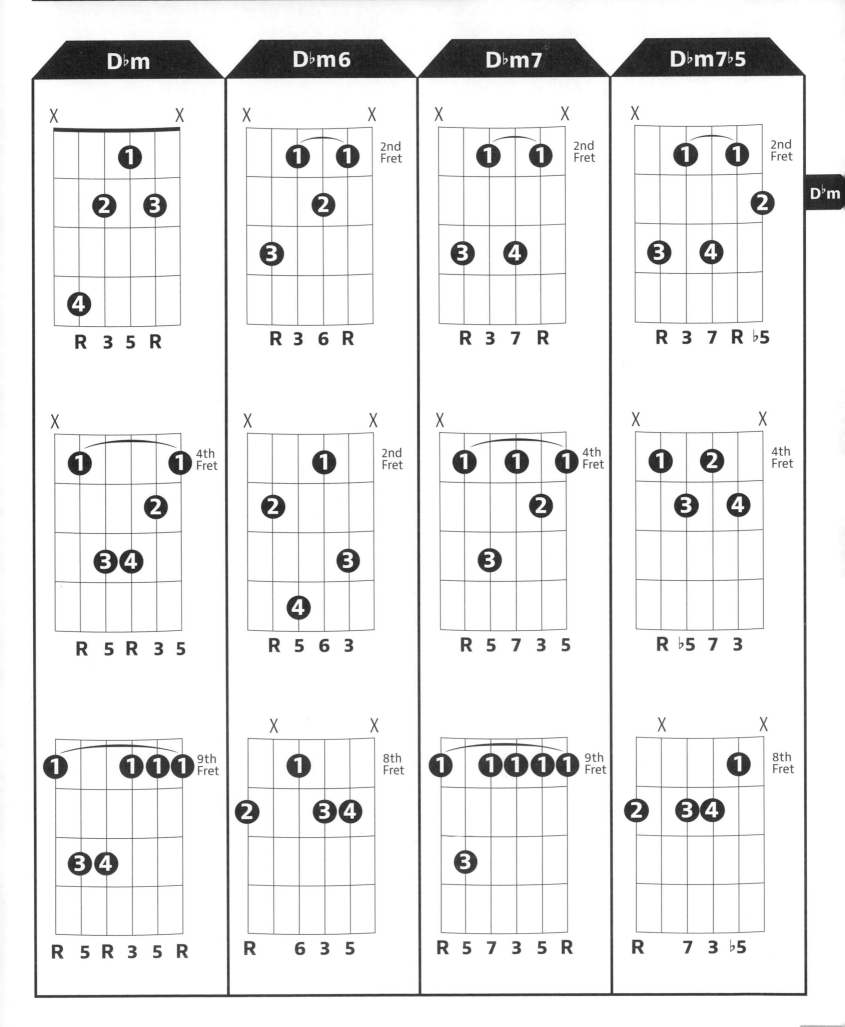

D♭m

D♭m6

D♭m7

D♭m7♭5

D♭m

D♭m

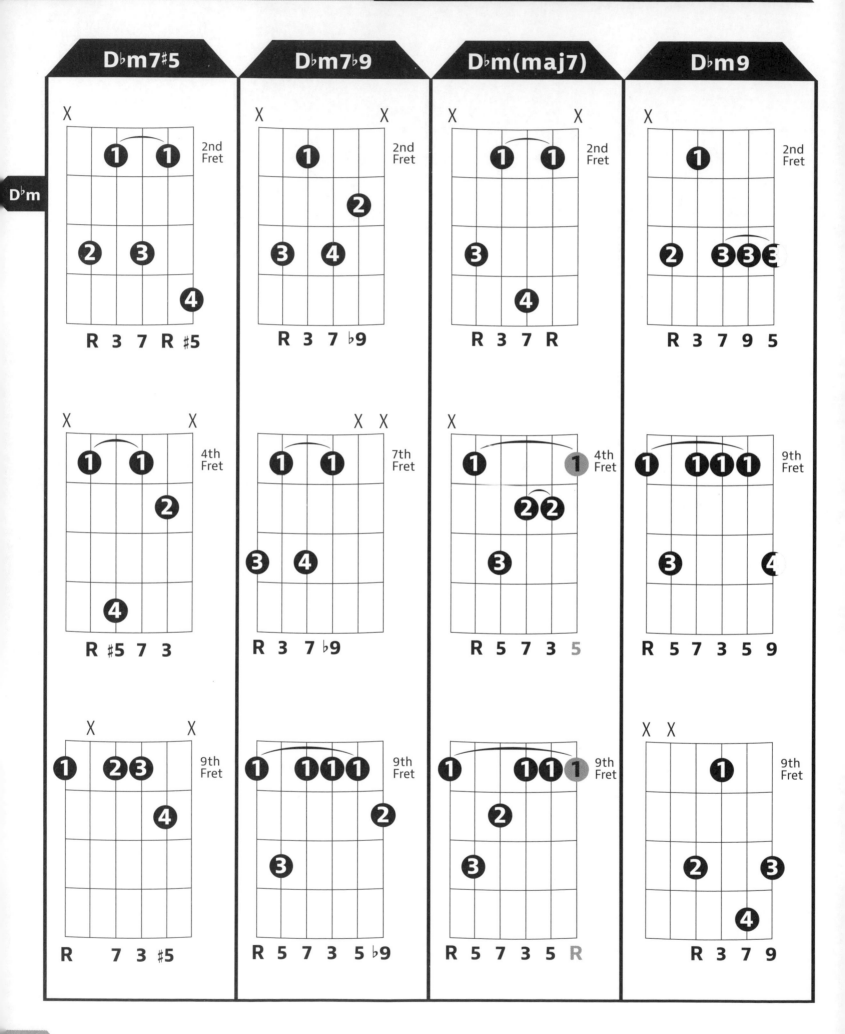

Db7

X   X

①   2nd Fret

②

③ ④

R 3 7 R

Db+

X   X

① ①

②

③

R 3 #5 R

Db7sus4

X

① ① 2nd Fret

③ ③ ③

R 4 7 R 4

Db7b5

X   X

① ② 4th Fret

③

④

R b5 7 3

X

① ① ① 4th Fret

③ ④

R 5 7 3 5

X   X

① ① 6th Fret

②

③

④

R 3 #5 R 3

X

① ① ① 4th Fret

③

④

R 5 7 4 5

X   X

① 8th Fret

② ③

④

R   7 3 b5

---

① ① ① ① 9th Fret

②

③

R 5 7 3 5 R

X X

① 9th Fret

② ③

④

R 3 #5 R

---

① ① ① ① 9th Fret

② ③

③ ④

R 5 7 4 5 R

X X

① 11th Fret

② ③

④

R b5 7 3

Db/C# Seventh

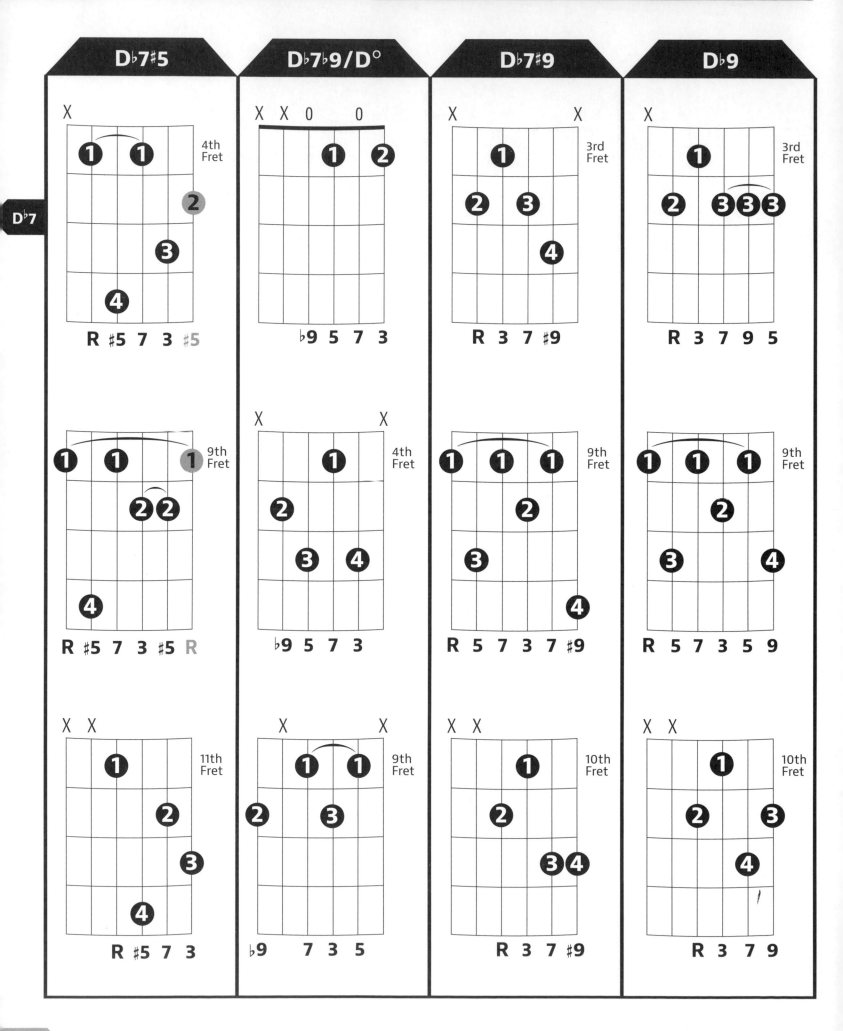

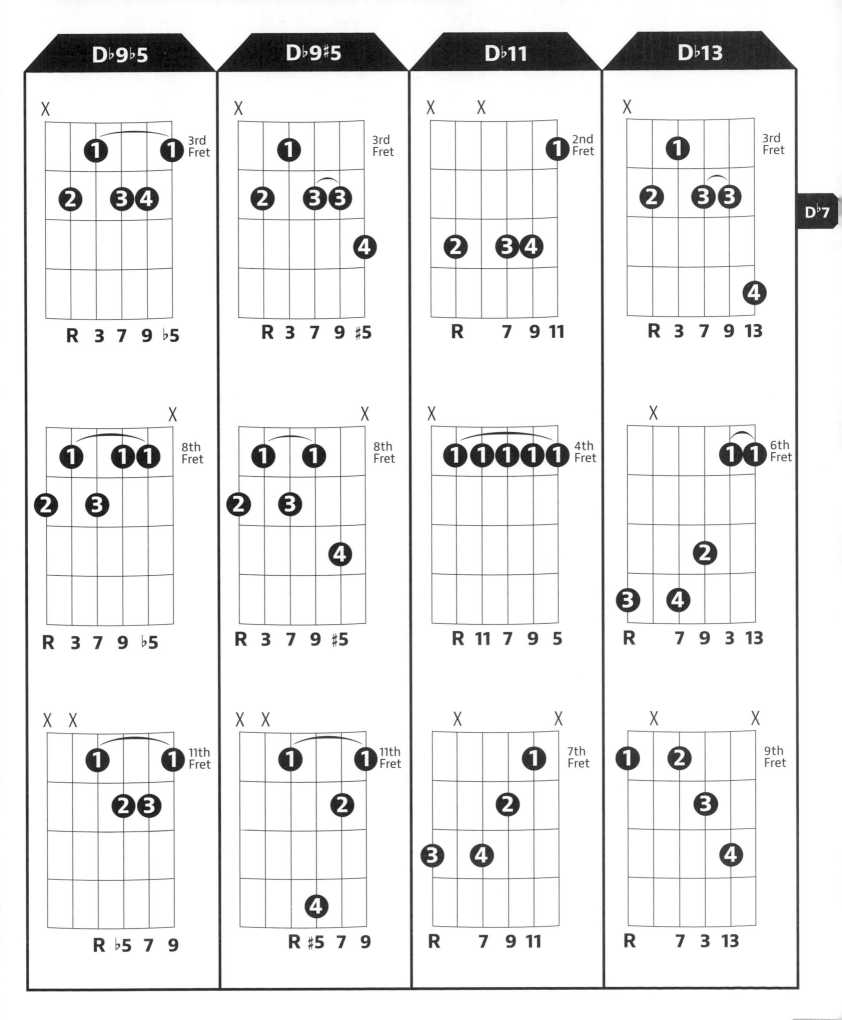

Db9b5

Db9#5

Db11

Db13

Db7

D

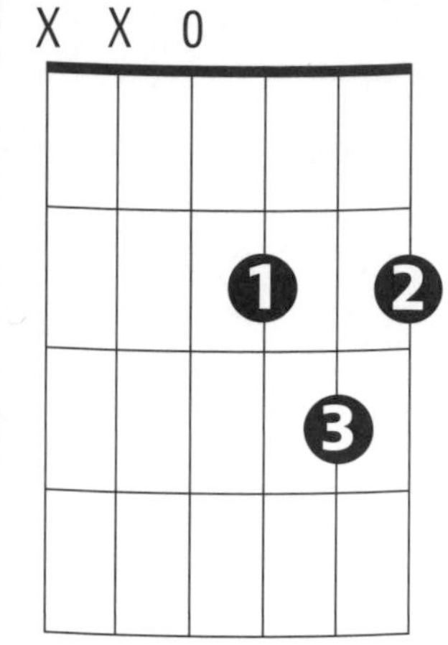

X X 0

R 5 R 3

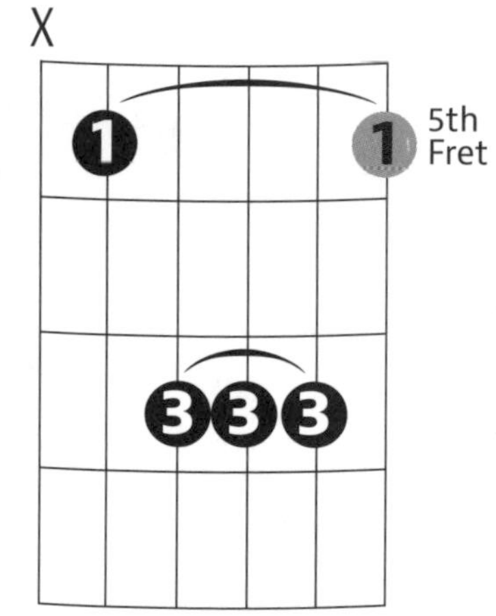

X

R 5 7 3 5

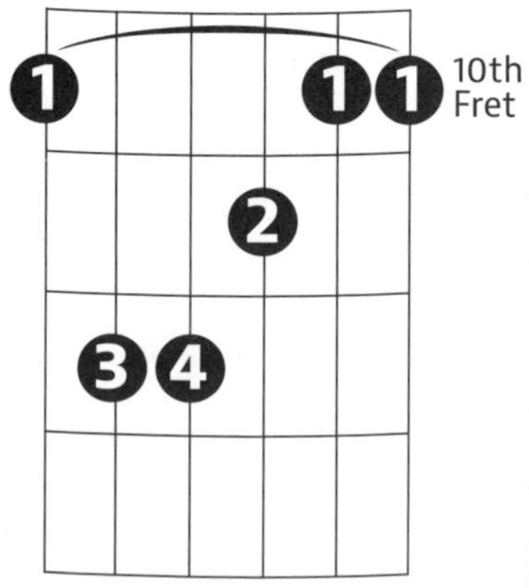

R 5 R 3 5 R

D6

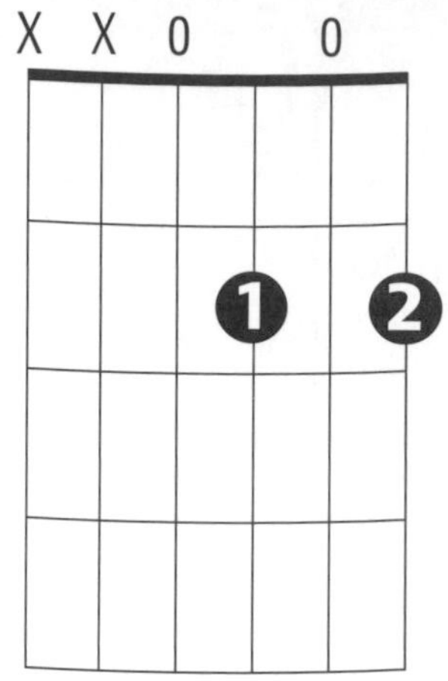

X X 0 0

R 5 6 3

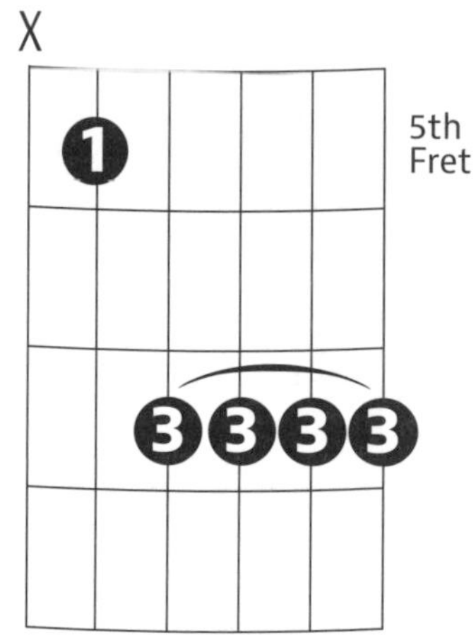

X

R 5 R 3 6

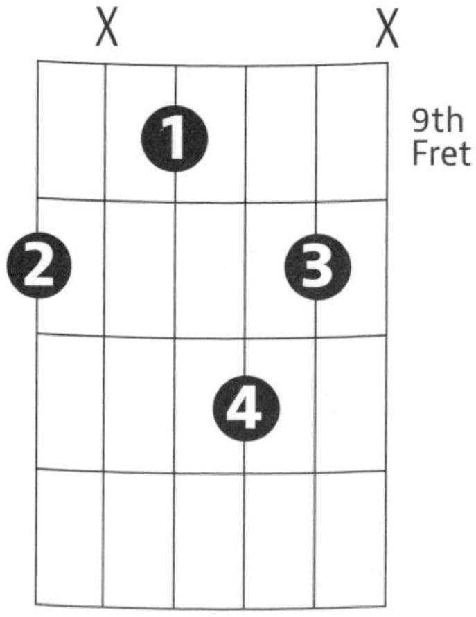

X   X

R   6 3 5

Dmaj7

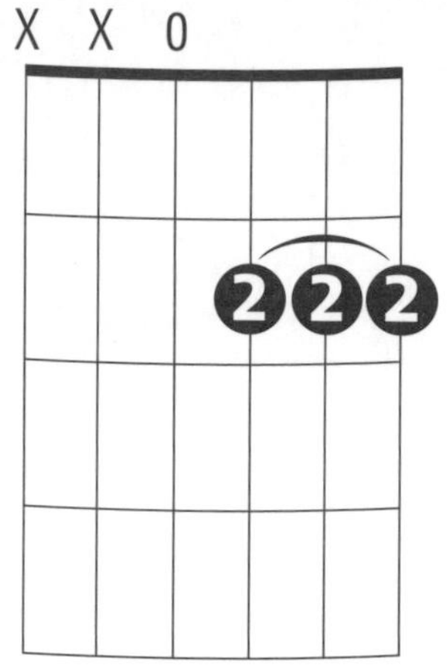

X X 0

R 5 7 3

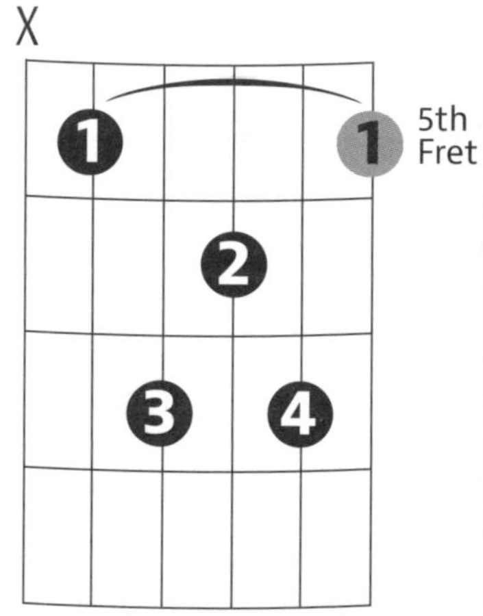

X

R 5 7 3 5

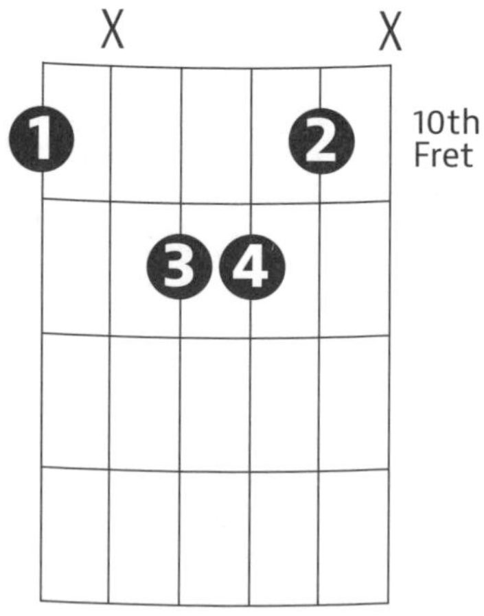

X   X

R   7 3 5

Dsus4

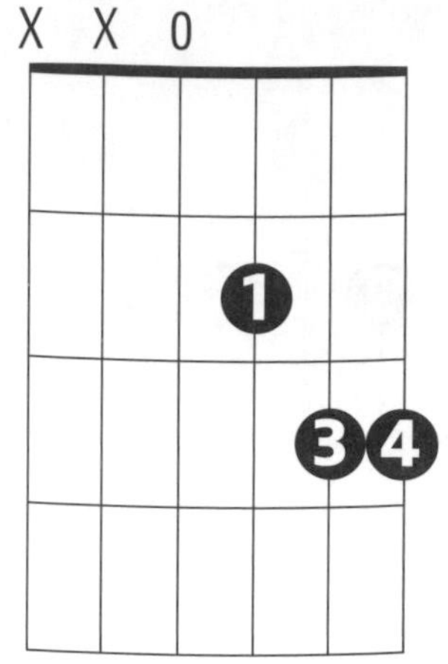

X X 0

R 5 R 4

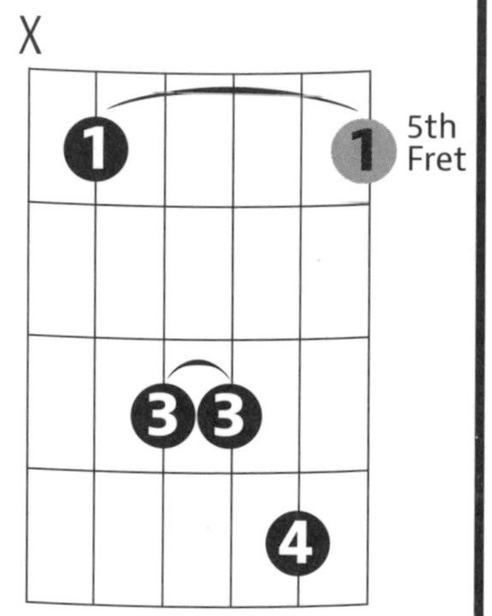

X

R 5 R 4 5

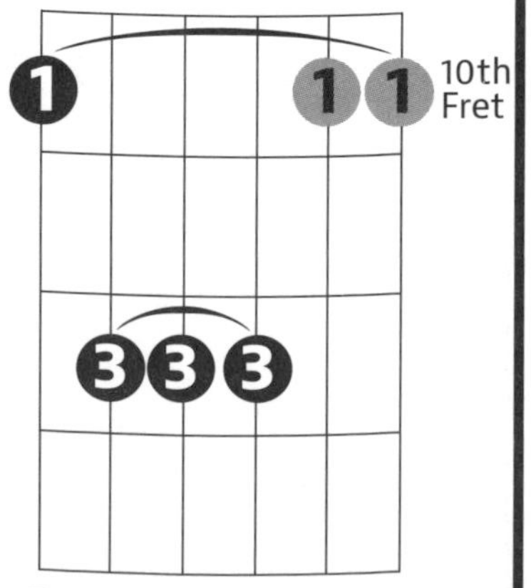

R 5 R 4 5 R

5th Fret (for all second-row diagrams)

10th Fret / 9th Fret / 10th Fret (for third-row diagrams)

Minor   D

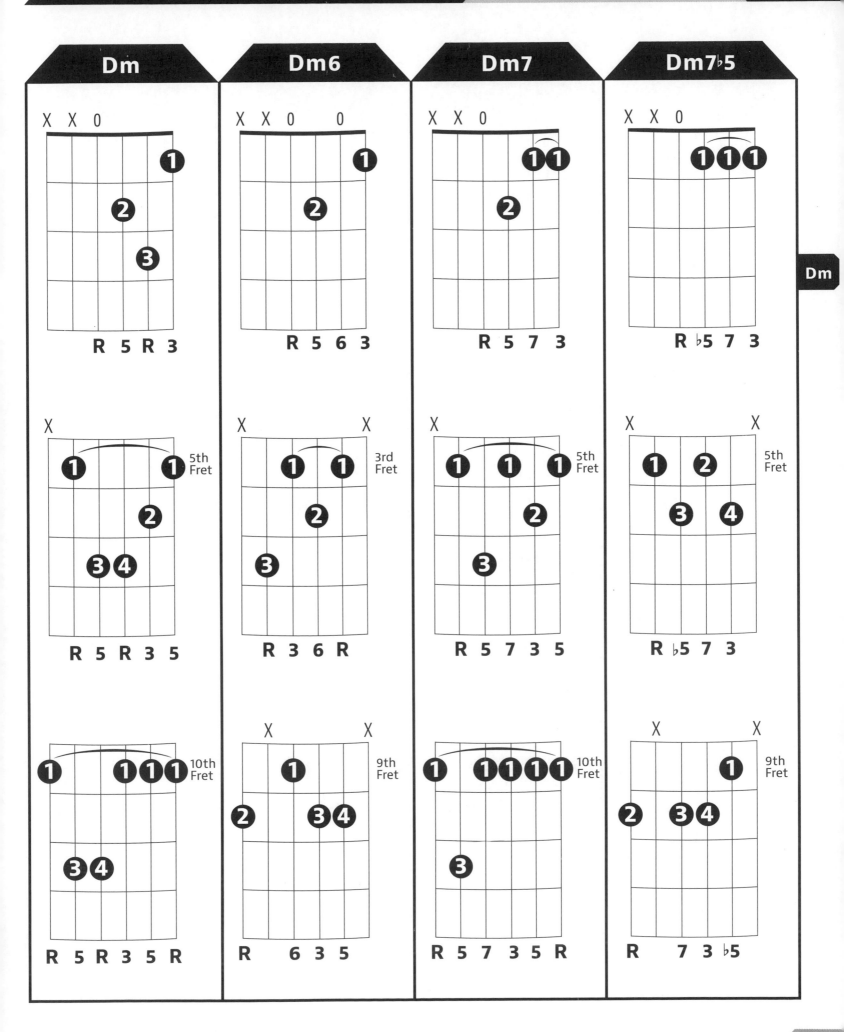

Dm   Dm6   Dm7   Dm7♭5

Dm

D Minor

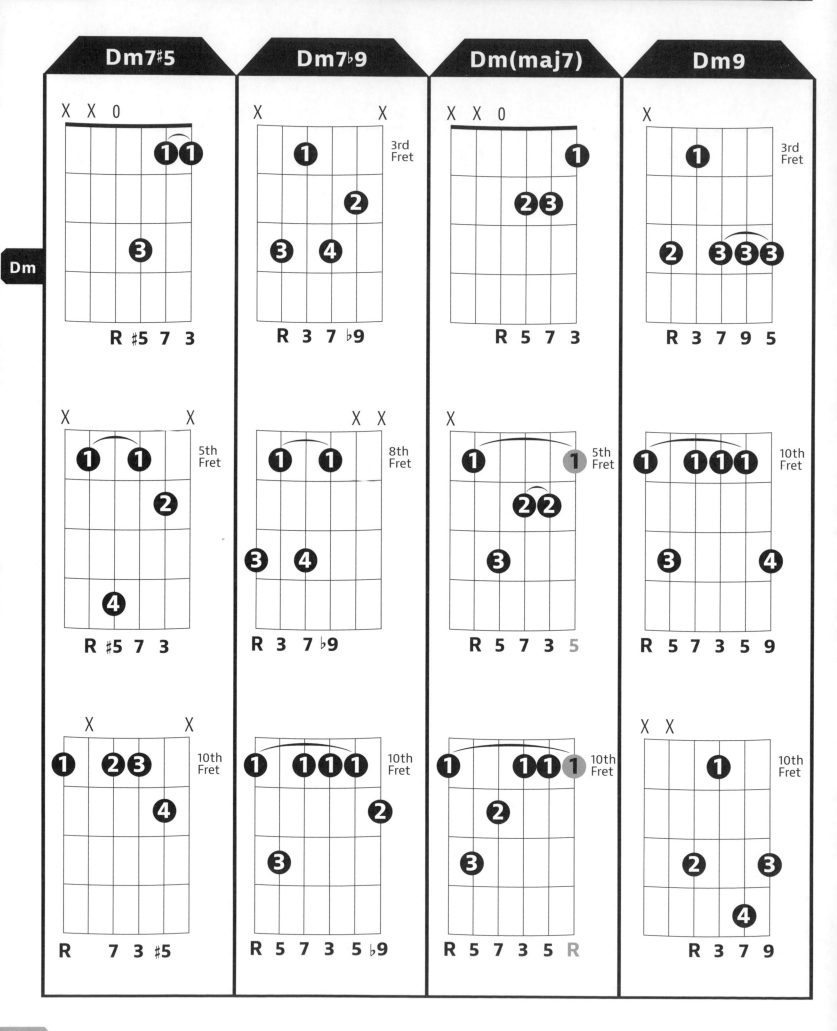

Dm

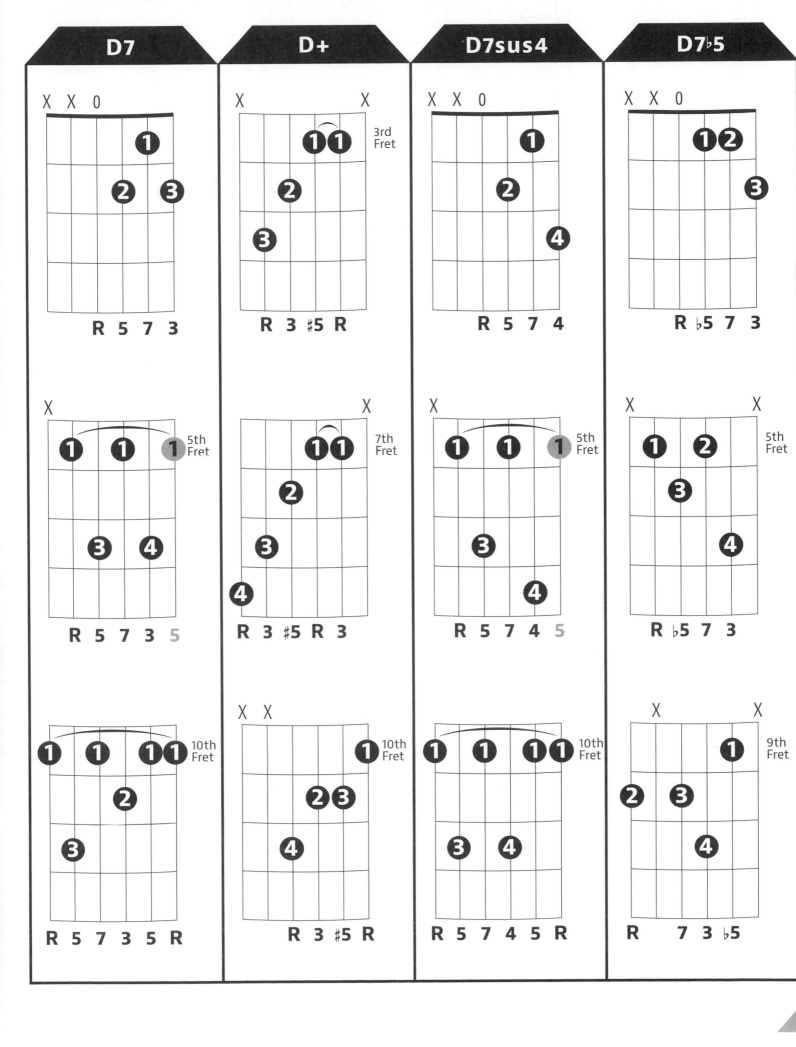

D7   D+   D7sus4   D7♭5

D7

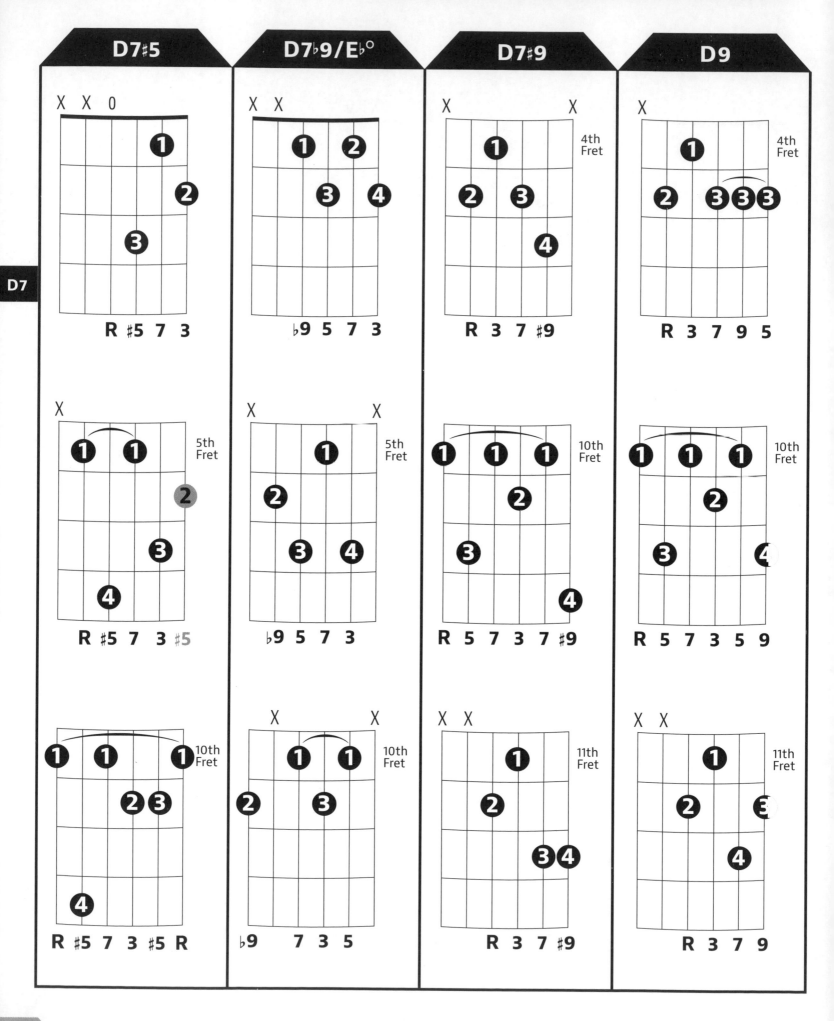

Seventh   **D**

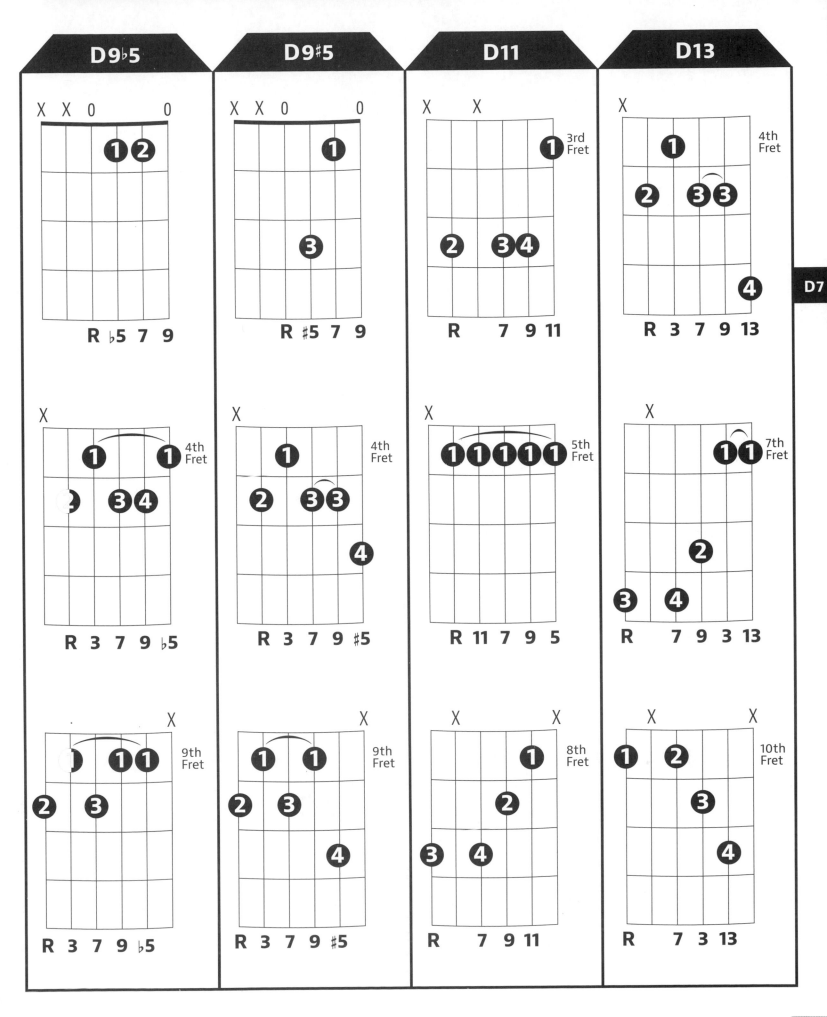

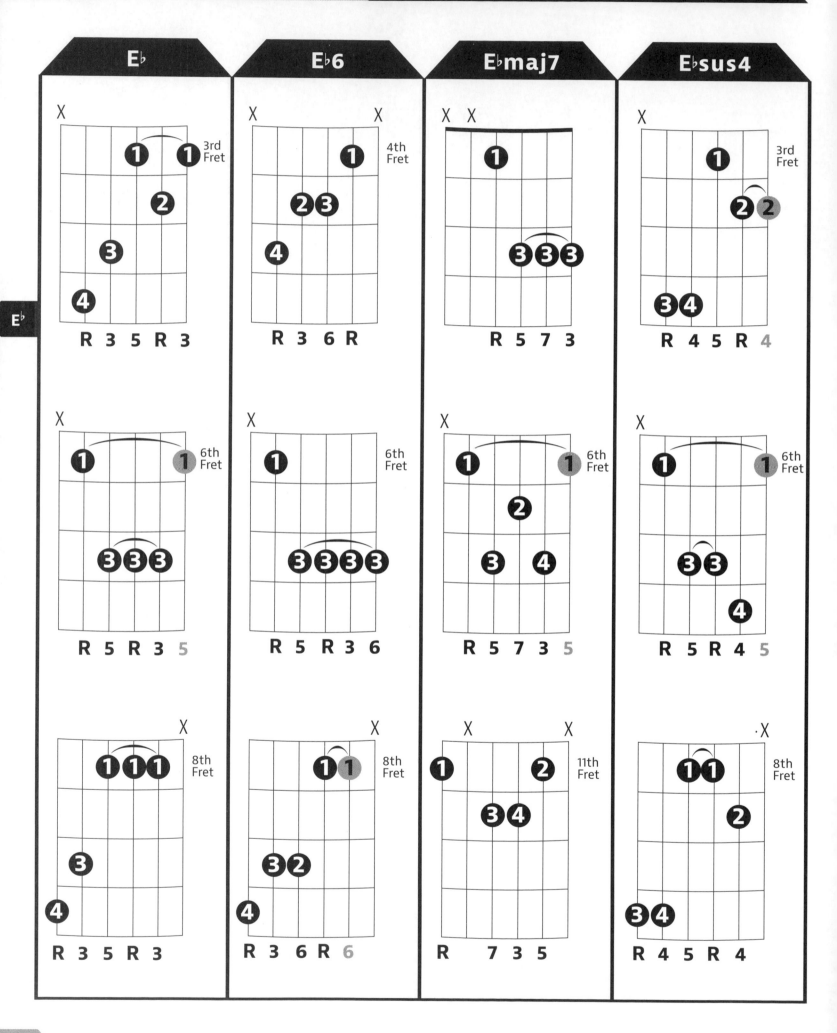

Minor

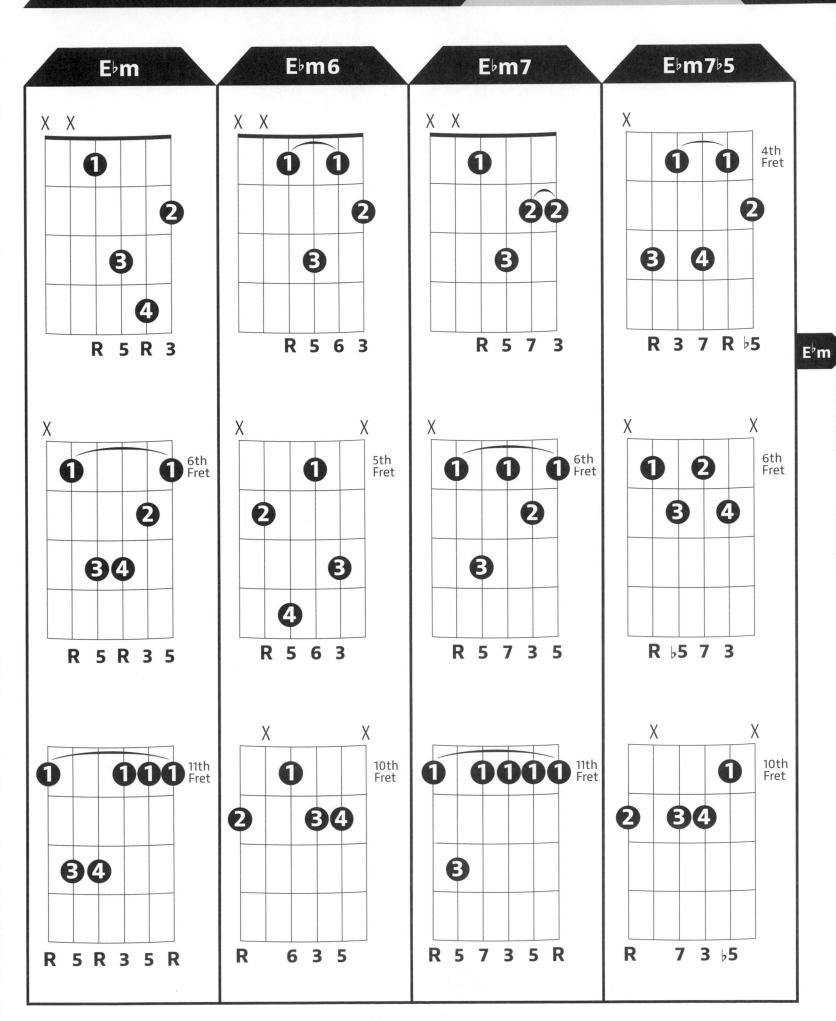

E♭/D♯ Minor

E♭m

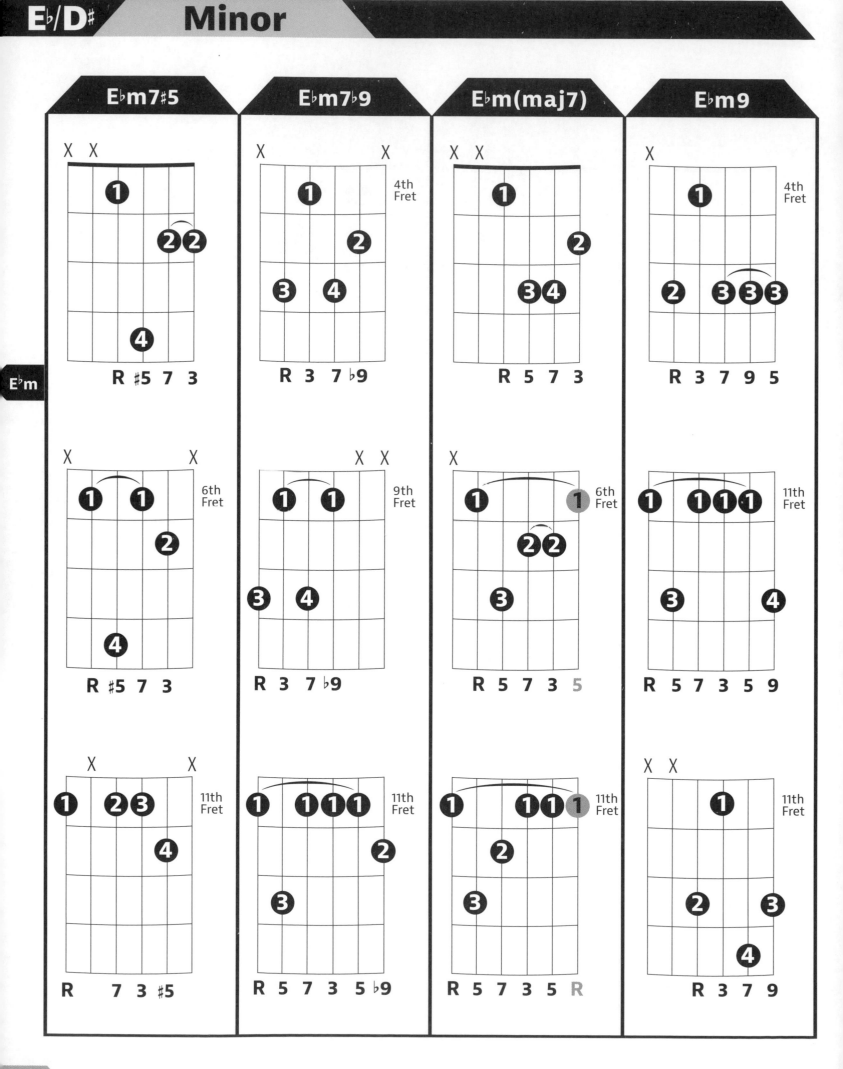

E♭m7♯5

R ♯5 7 3

R ♯5 7 3

R   7 3 ♯5

E♭m7♭9

4th Fret

R 3 7 ♭9

9th Fret

R 3 7 ♭9

11th Fret

R 5 7 3 5 ♭9

E♭m(maj7)

R 5 7 3

6th Fret

R 5 7 3 5

11th Fret

R 5 7 3 5 R

E♭m9

4th Fret

R 3 7 9 5

11th Fret

R 5 7 3 5 9

11th Fret

R 3 7 9

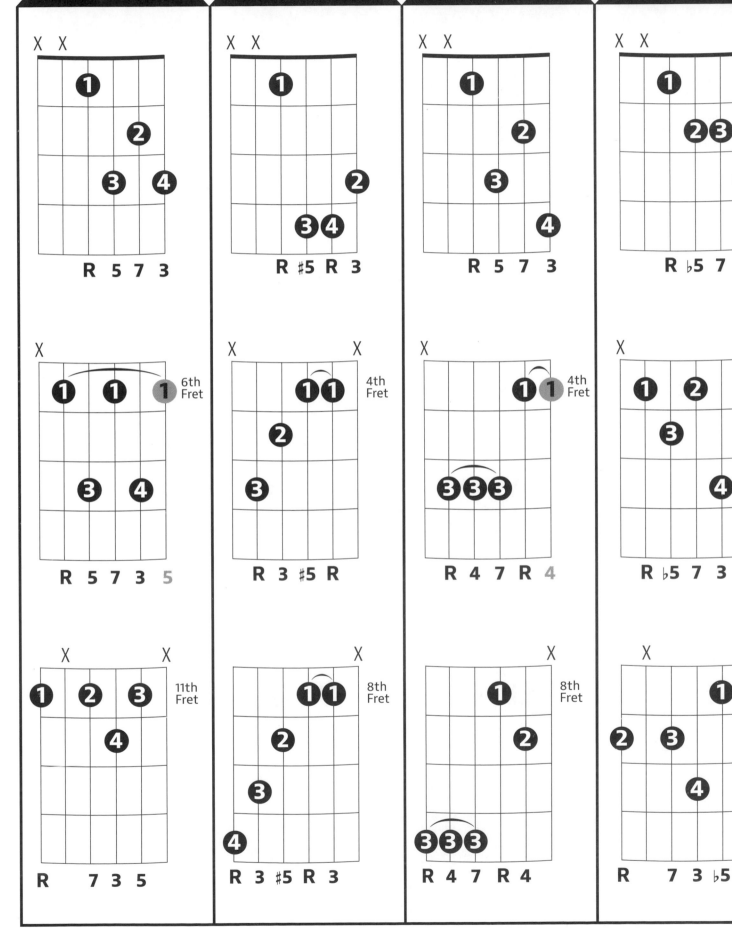

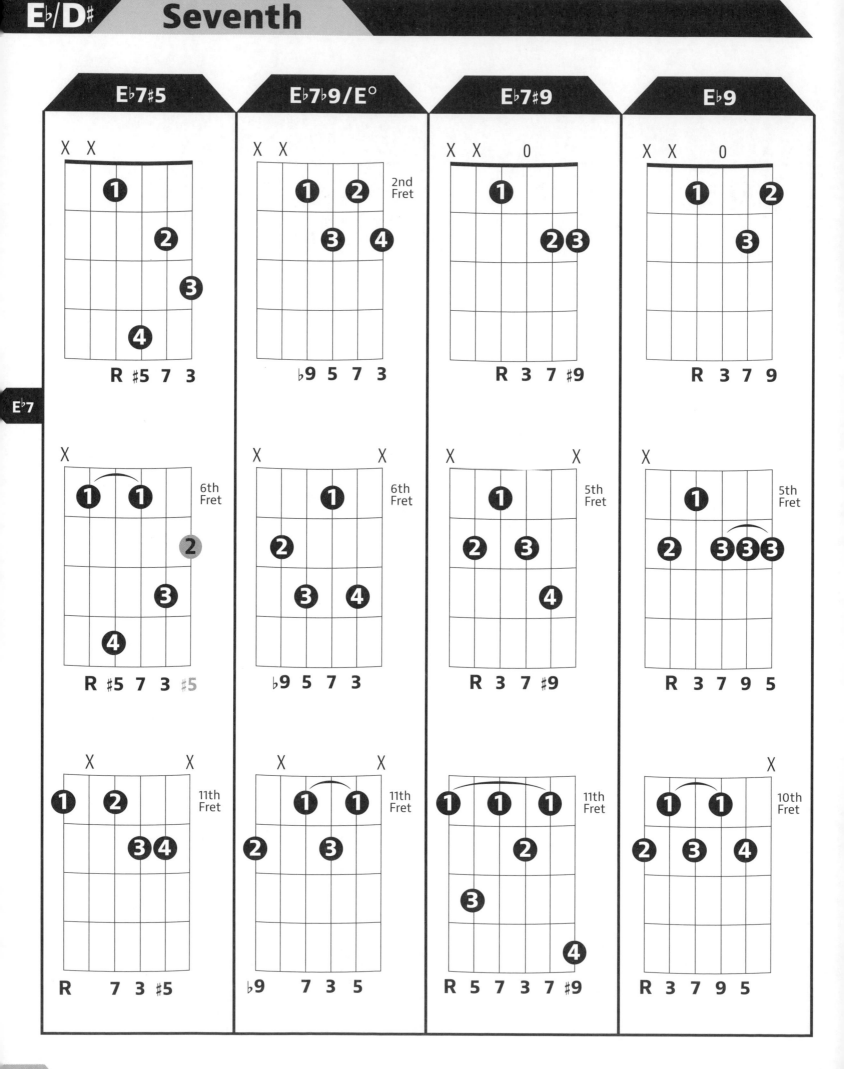

E♭7#5

R #5 7 3

R #5 7 3 #5

R 7 3 #5

E♭7♭9/E°

♭9 5 7 3

♭9 5 7 3

♭9 7 3 5

E♭7#9

R 3 7 #9

R 3 7 #9

R 5 7 3 7 #9

E♭9

R 3 7 9

R 3 7 9 5

R 3 7 9 5

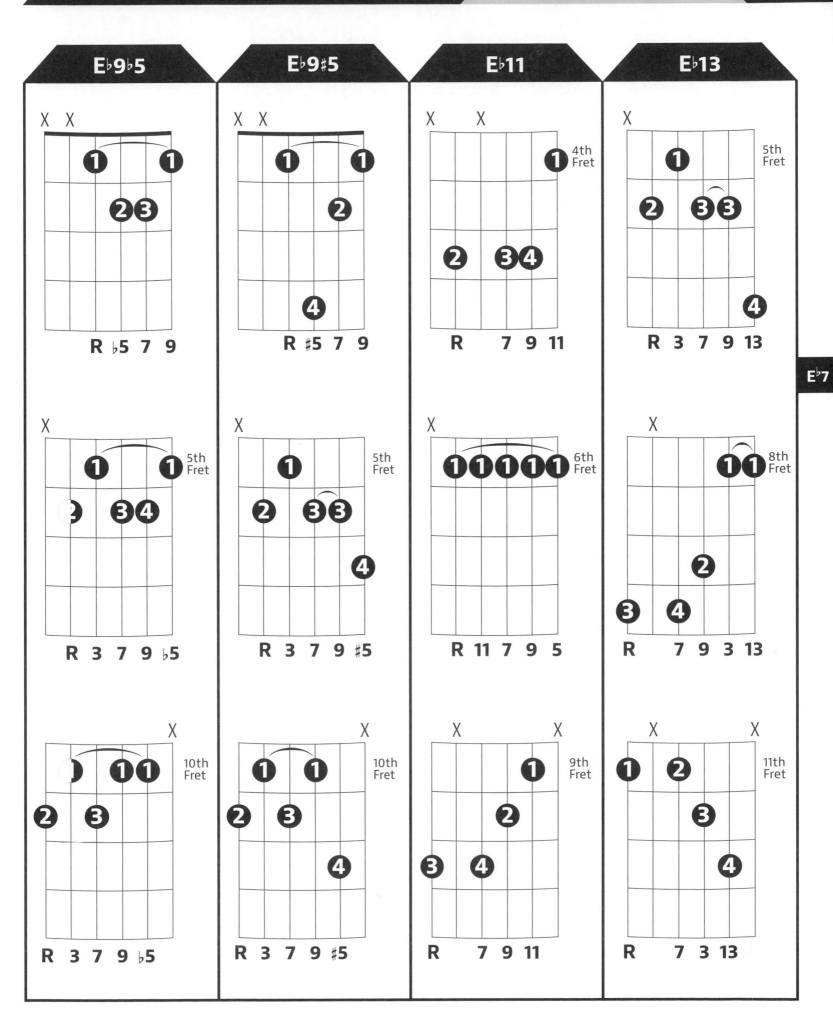

E♭9♭5 · R ♭5 7 9

E♭9#5 · R #5 7 9

E♭11 · 4th Fret · R 7 9 11

E♭13 · 5th Fret · R 3 7 9 13

E♭7

E♭9♭5 · 5th Fret · R 3 7 9 ♭5

E♭9#5 · 5th Fret · R 3 7 9 #5

E♭11 · 6th Fret · R 11 7 9 5

E♭13 · 8th Fret · R 7 9 3 13

E♭9♭5 · 10th Fret · R 3 7 9 ♭5

E♭9#5 · 10th Fret · R 3 7 9 #5

E♭11 · 9th Fret · R 7 9 11

E♭13 · 11th Fret · R 7 3 13

E   Major

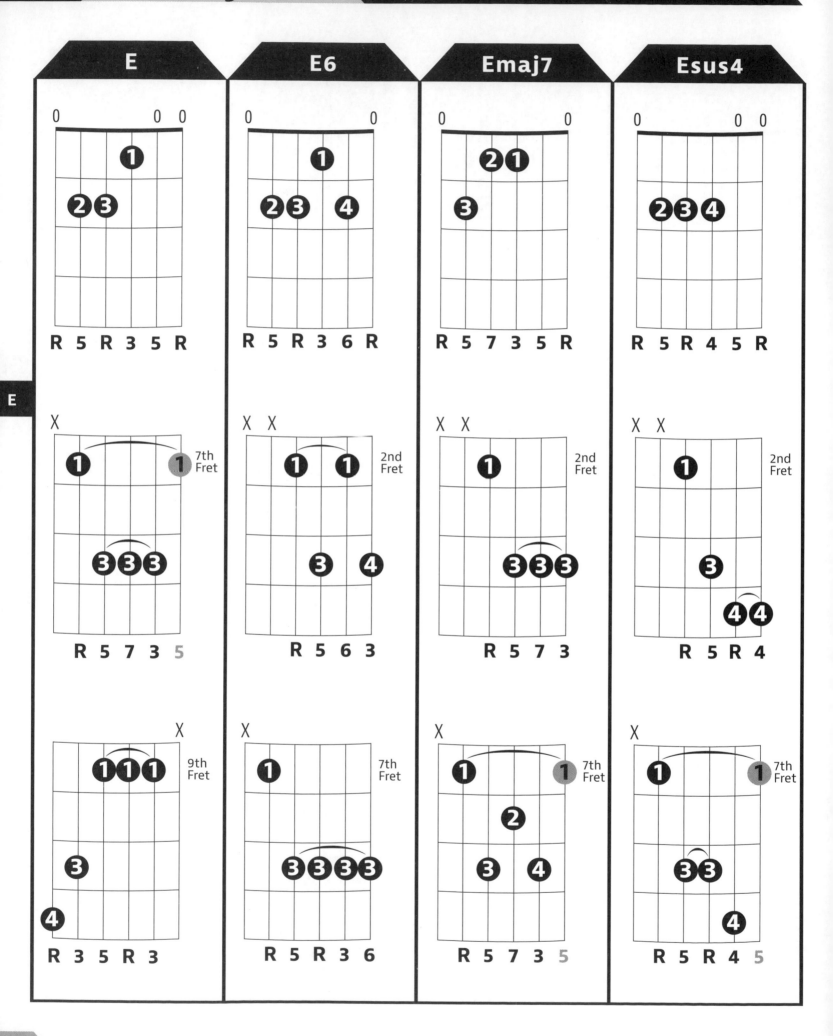

Minor E

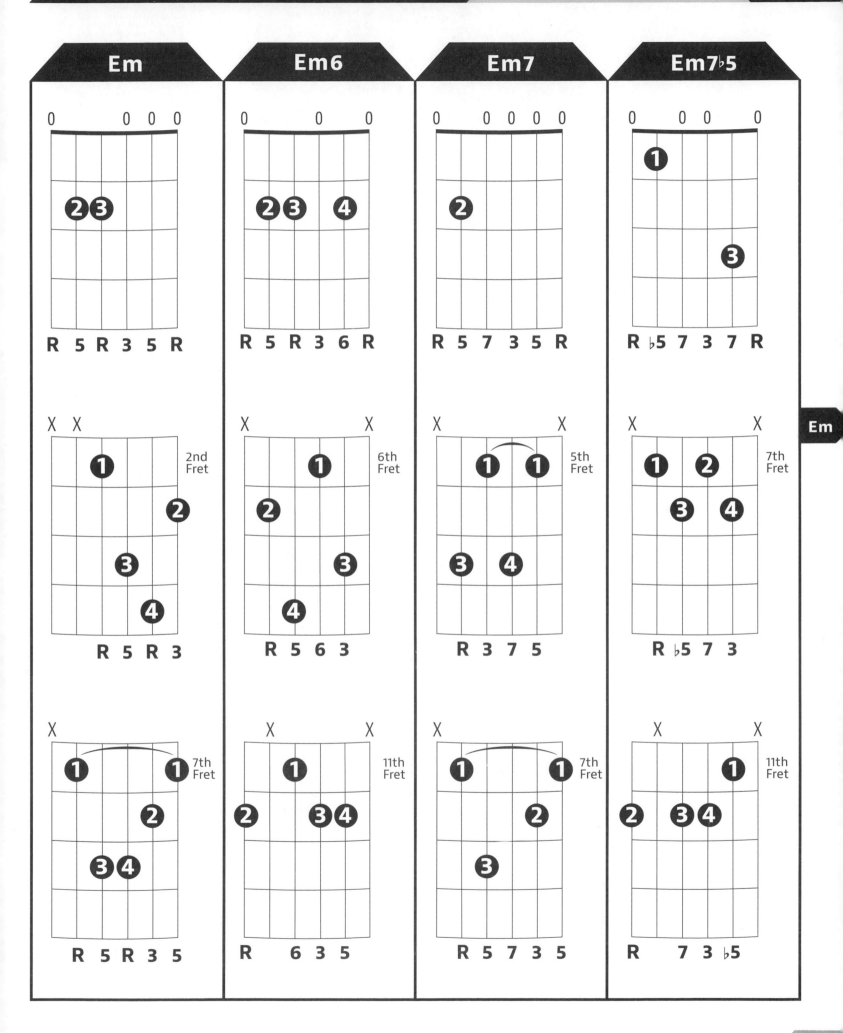

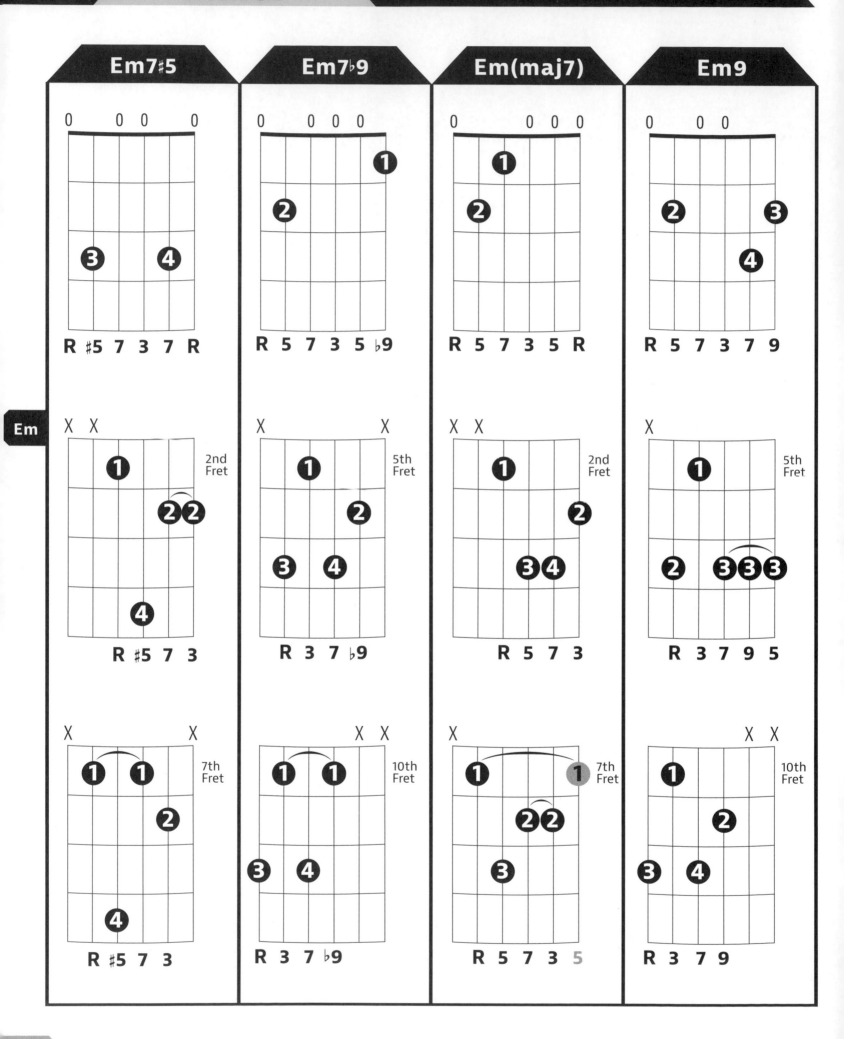

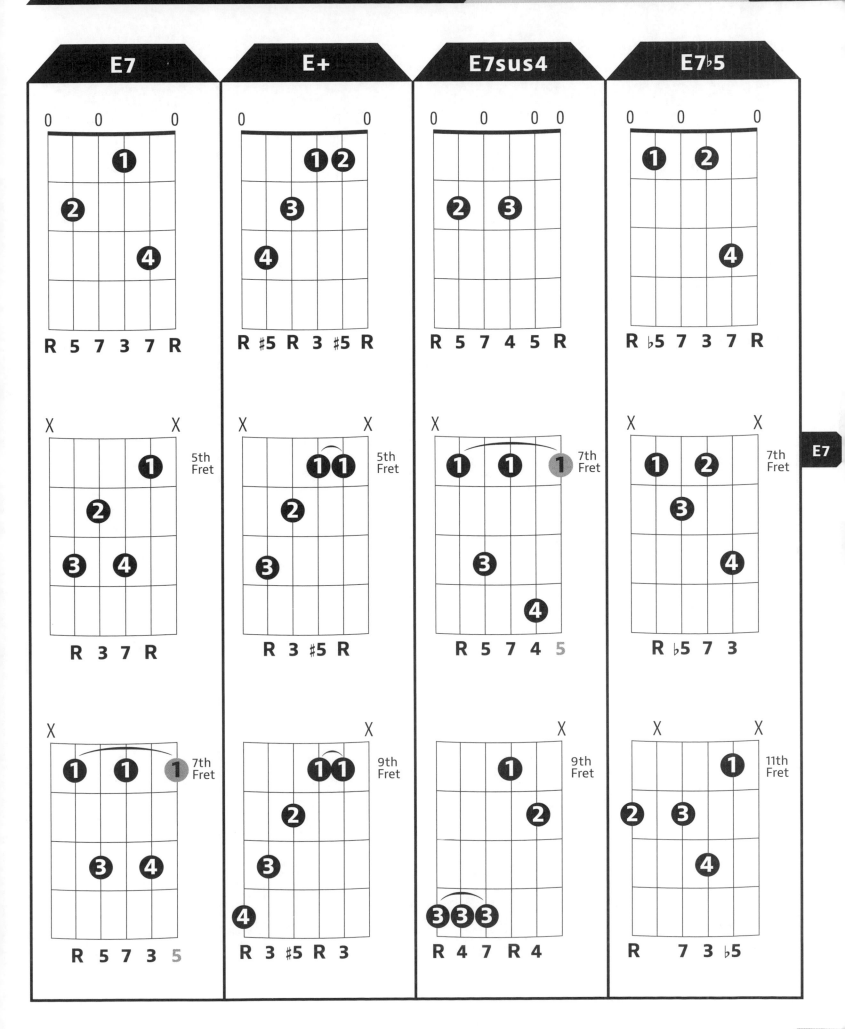

E7

R 5 7 3 7 R

R 3 7 R

R 5 7 3 5

E+

R ♯5 R 3 ♯5 R

R 3 ♯5 R

R 3 ♯5 R 3

E7sus4

R 5 7 4 5 R

R 5 7 4 5

R 4 7 R 4

E7♭5

R ♭5 7 3 7 R

R ♭5 7 3

R 7 3 ♭5

E7

E   Seventh

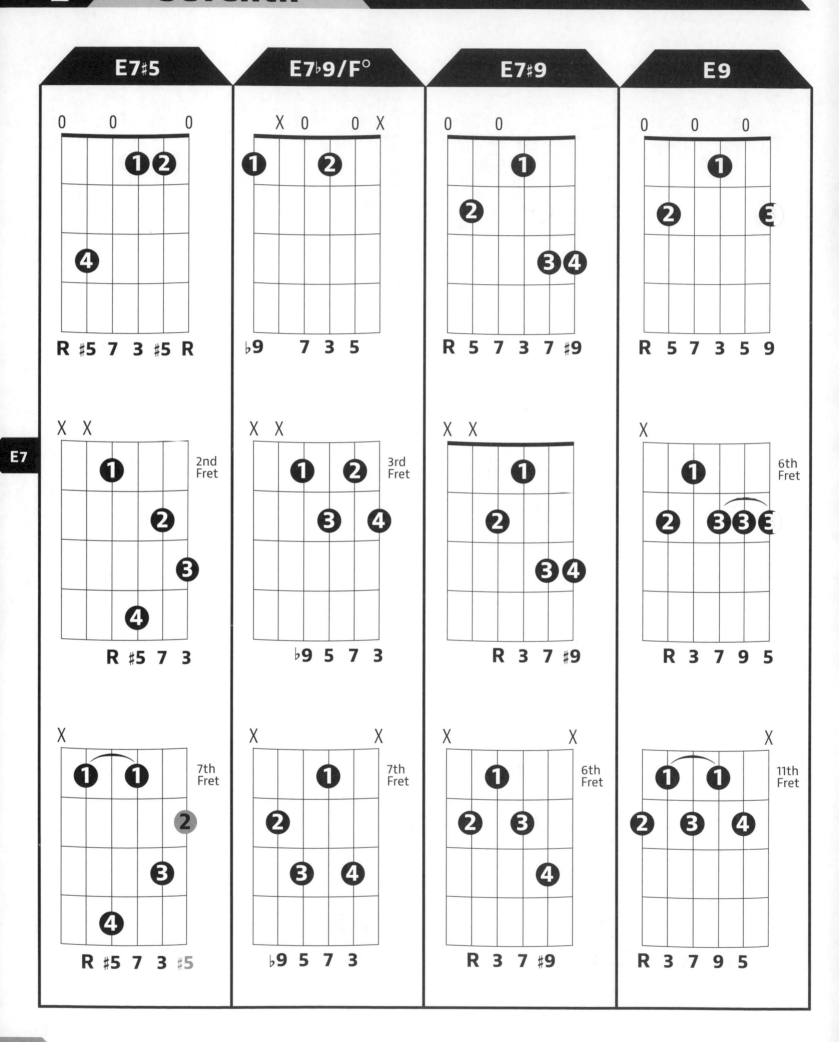

E7#5

R   #5   7   3   #5   R

R   #5   7   3   (2nd Fret)

R   #5   7   3   #5   (7th Fret)

E7♭9/F°

♭9   7   3   5

♭9   5   7   3   (3rd Fret)

♭9   5   7   3   (7th Fret)

E7#9

R   5   7   3   7   #9

R   3   7   #9   (6th Fret)

R   3   7   #9   (6th Fret)

E9

R   5   7   3   5   9

R   3   7   9   5   (6th Fret)

R   3   7   9   5   (11th Fret)

E7

50

Seventh   E

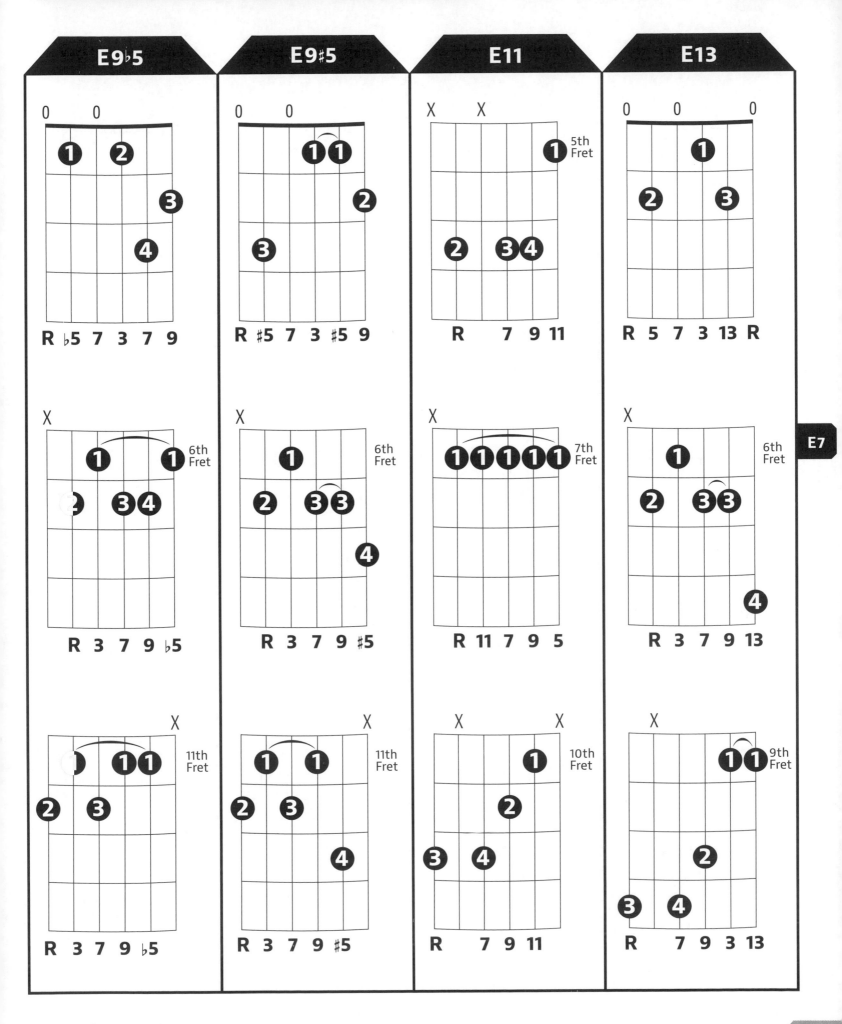

Major

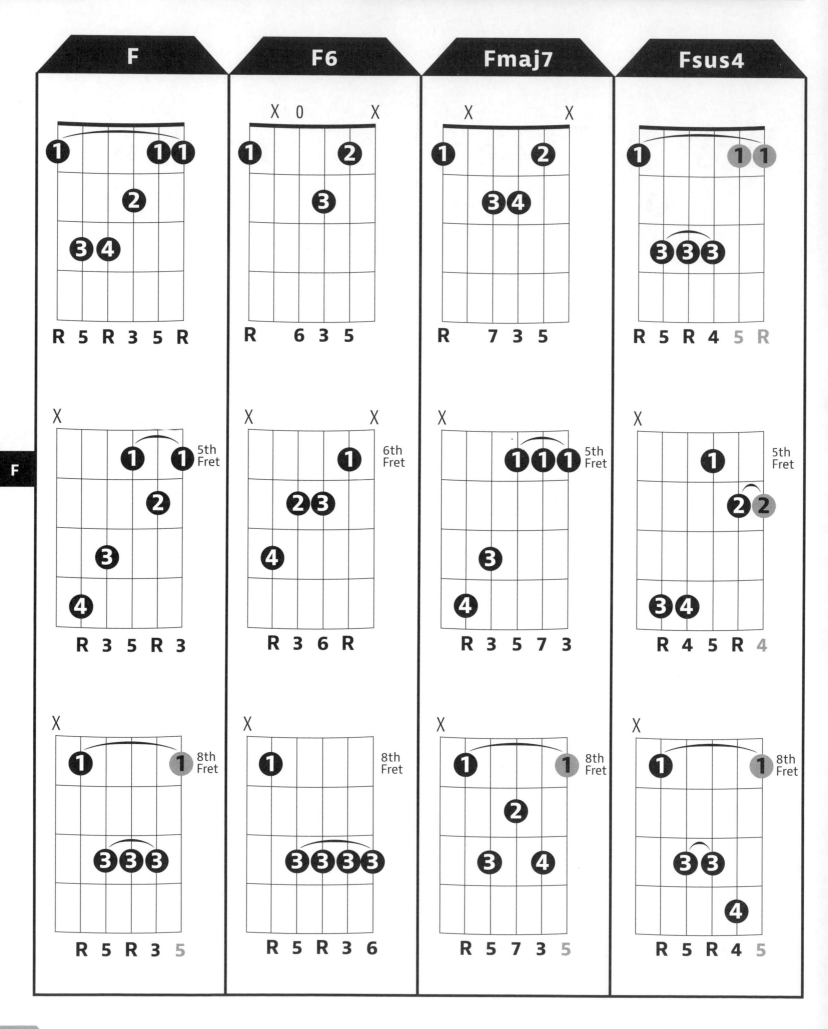

F

R 5 R 3 5 R

F6

X 0 X

R 6 3 5

Fmaj7

X X

R 7 3 5

Fsus4

R 5 R 4 5 R

X

5th Fret

R 3 5 R 3

X X

6th Fret

R 3 6 R

X

5th Fret

R 3 5 7 3

X

5th Fret

R 4 5 R 4

X

8th Fret

R 5 R 3 5

X

8th Fret

R 5 R 3 6

X

8th Fret

R 5 7 3 5

X

8th Fret

R 5 R 4 5

Minor   F

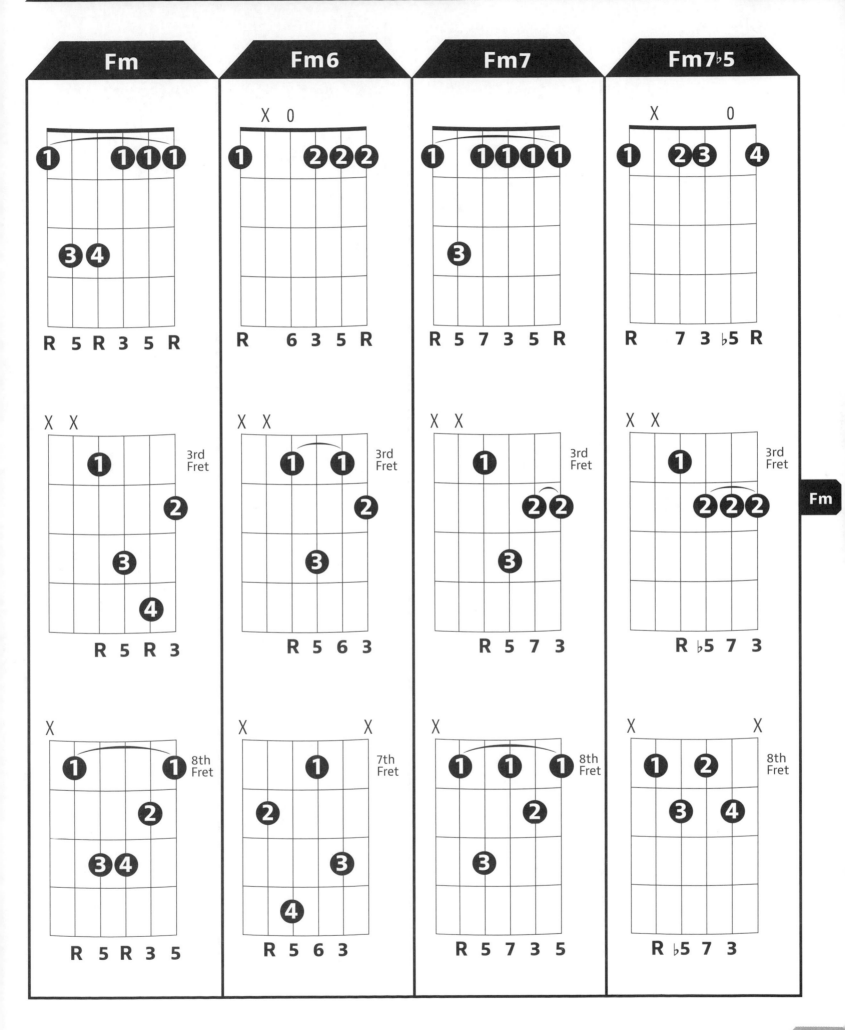

F Minor

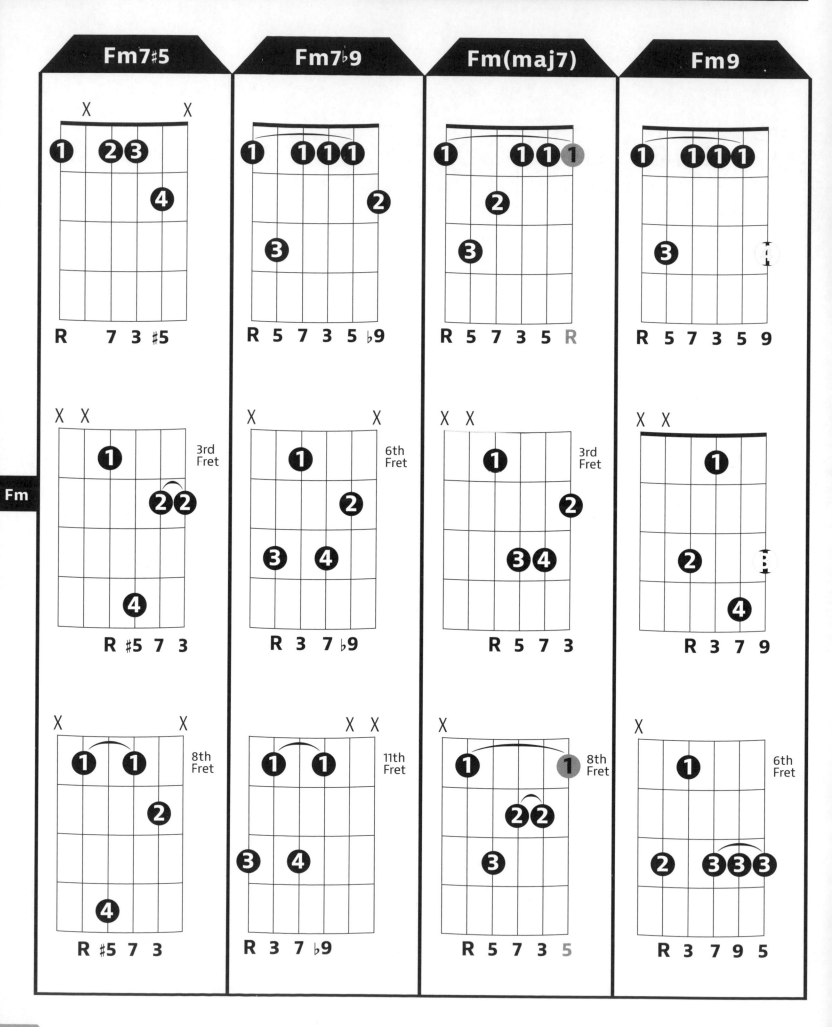

Seventh   F

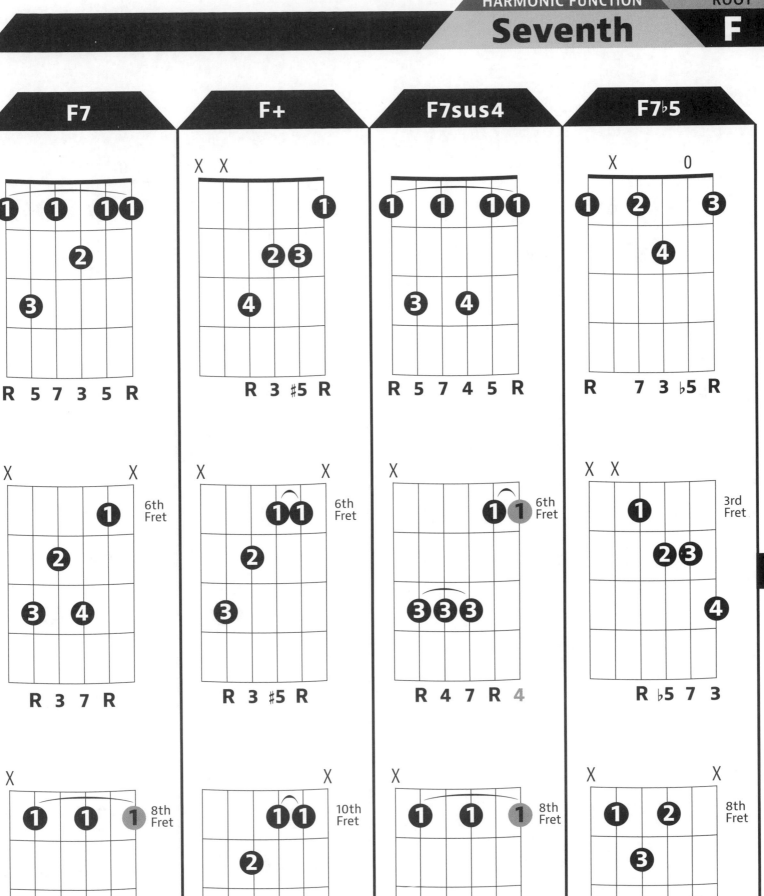

F Seventh

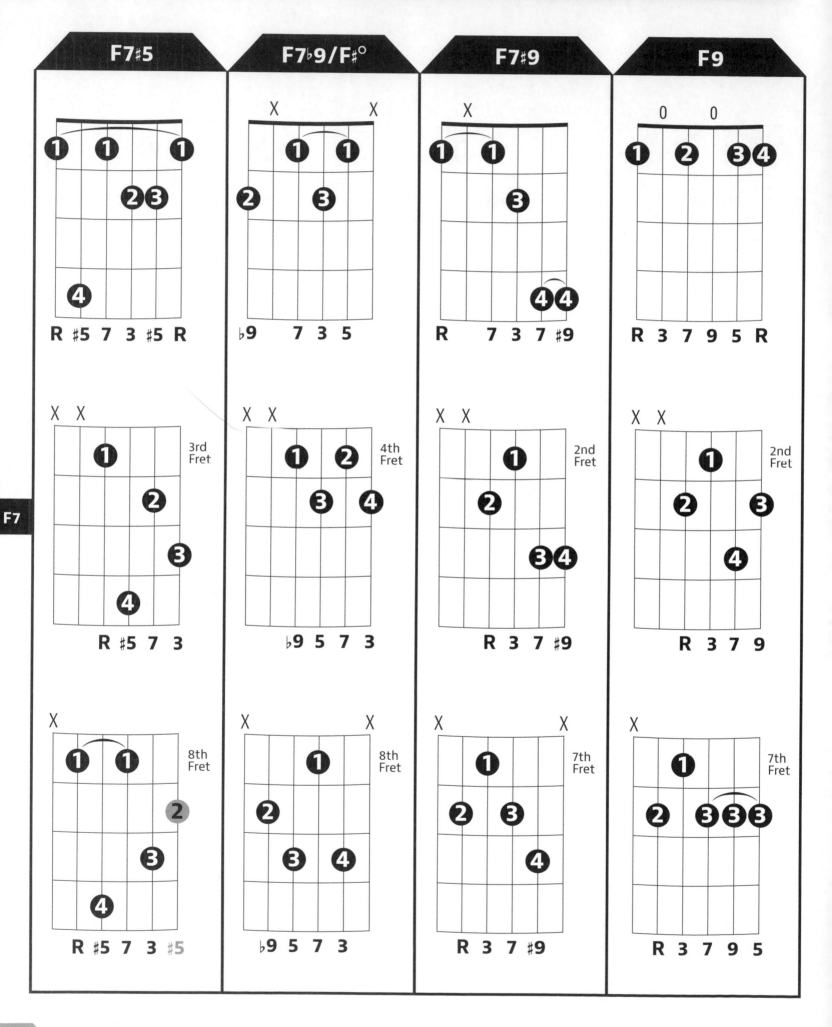

Seventh   F

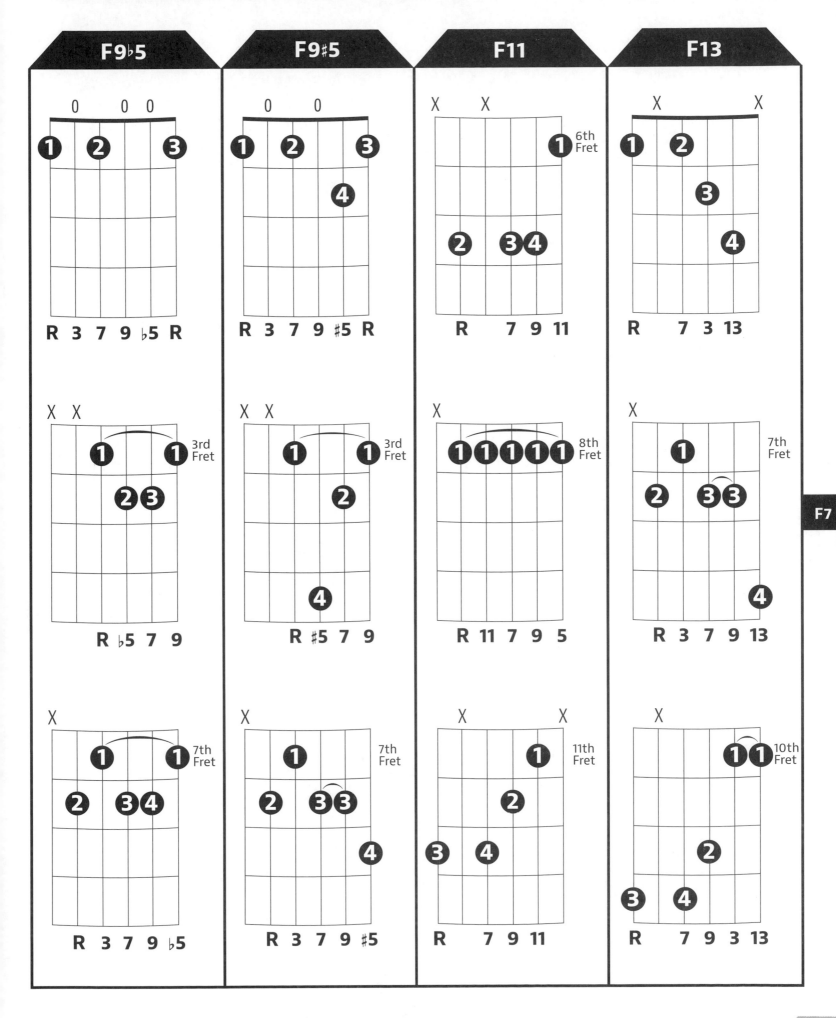

F9♭5

R 3 7 9 ♭5 R

R ♭5 7 9

R 3 7 9 ♭5

F9♯5

R 3 7 9 ♯5 R

R ♯5 7 9

R 3 7 9 ♯5

F11

6th Fret

R 7 9 11

8th Fret

R 11 7 9 5

11th Fret

R 7 9 11

F13

R 7 3 13

7th Fret

R 3 7 9 13

10th Fret

R 7 9 3 13

F7

F#/G♭ Major

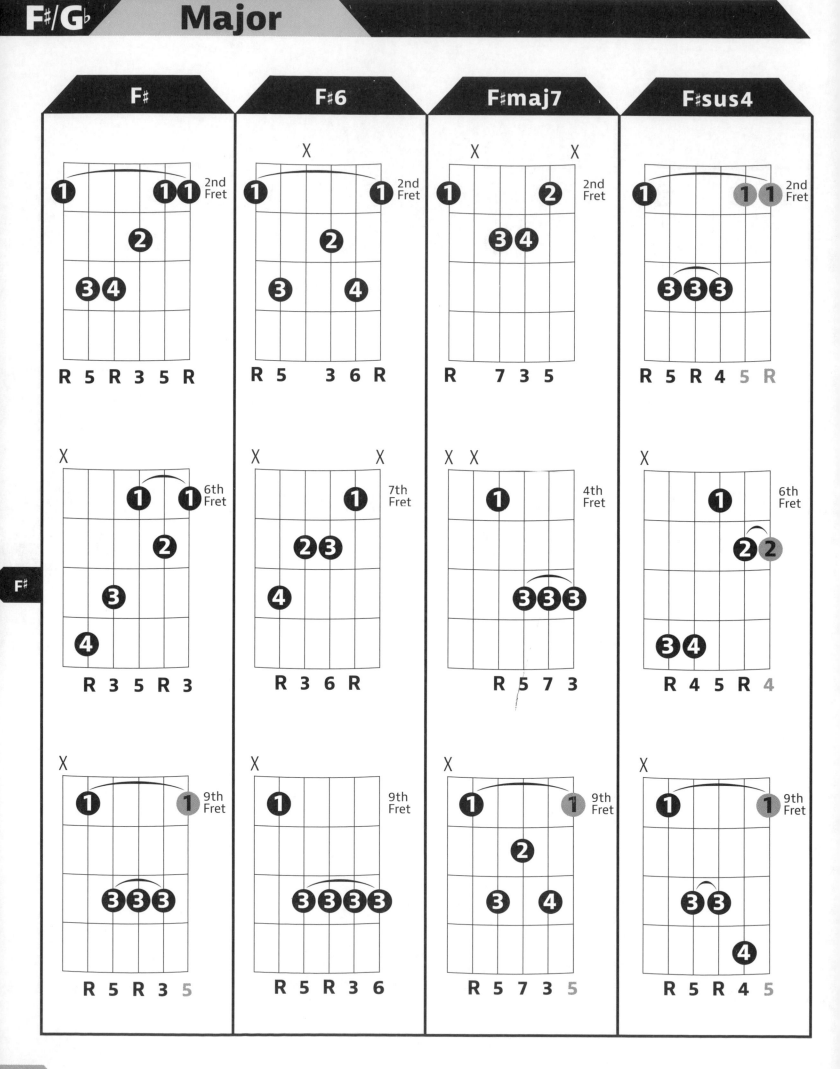

Minor   F♯/G♭

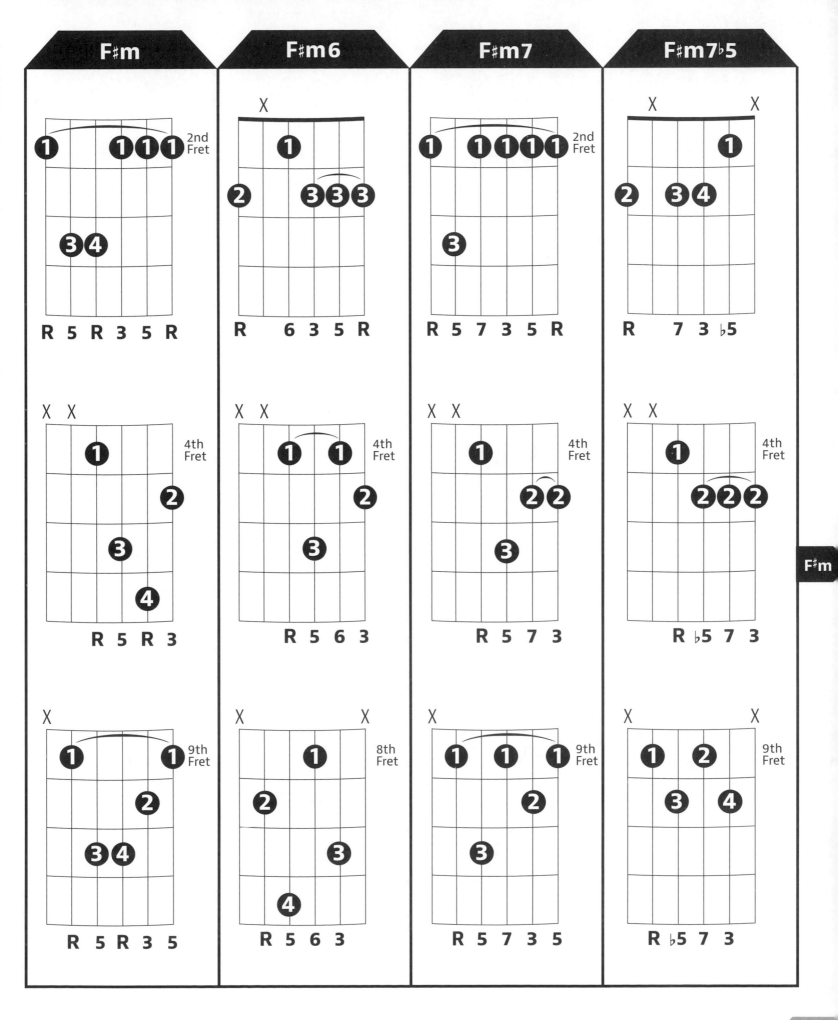

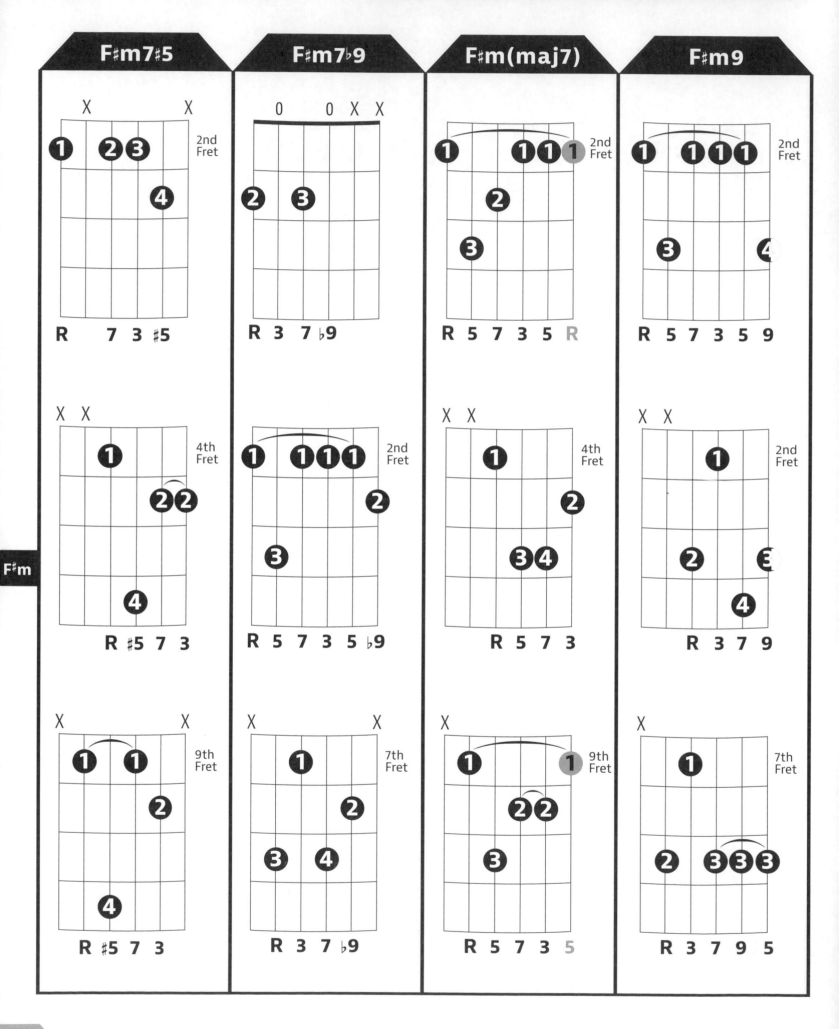

Seventh

F#/Gb

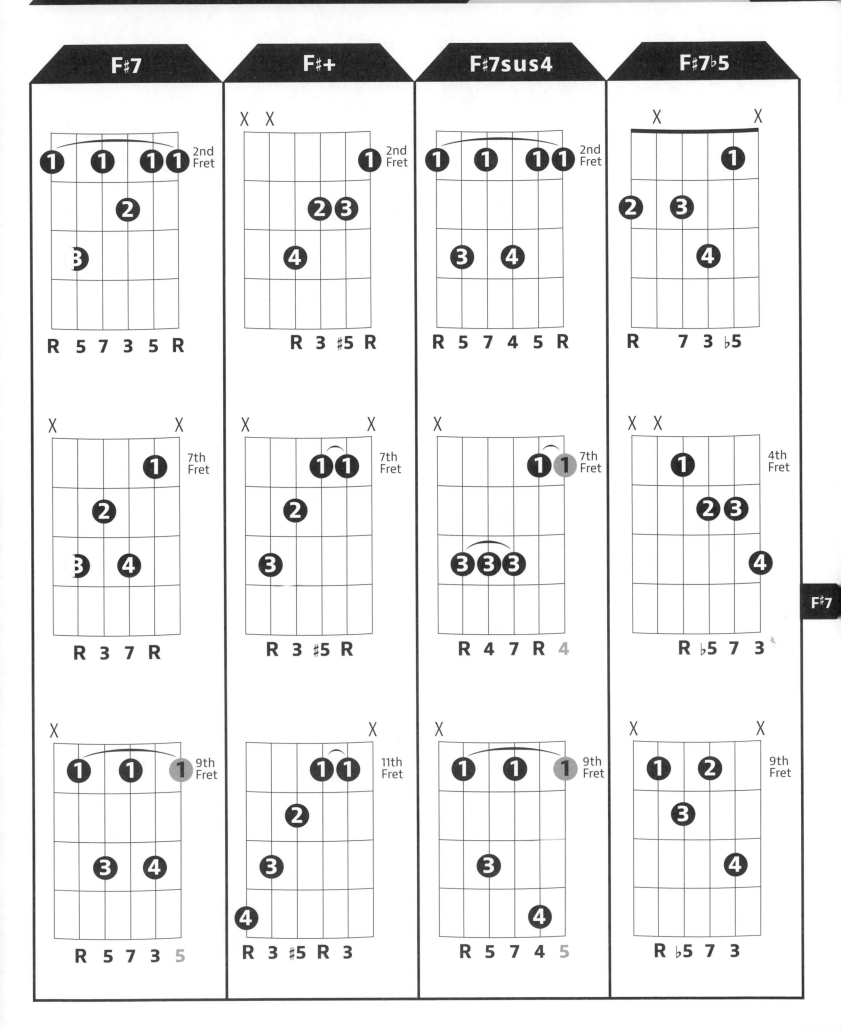

F#7

R 5 7 3 5 R

R 3 7 R

R 5 7 3 5

F#+

R 3 #5 R

R 3 #5 R

R 3 #5 R 3

F#7sus4

R 5 7 4 5 R

R 4 7 R 4

R 5 7 4 5

F#7b5

R 7 3 b5

R b5 7 3

R b5 7 3

F#7

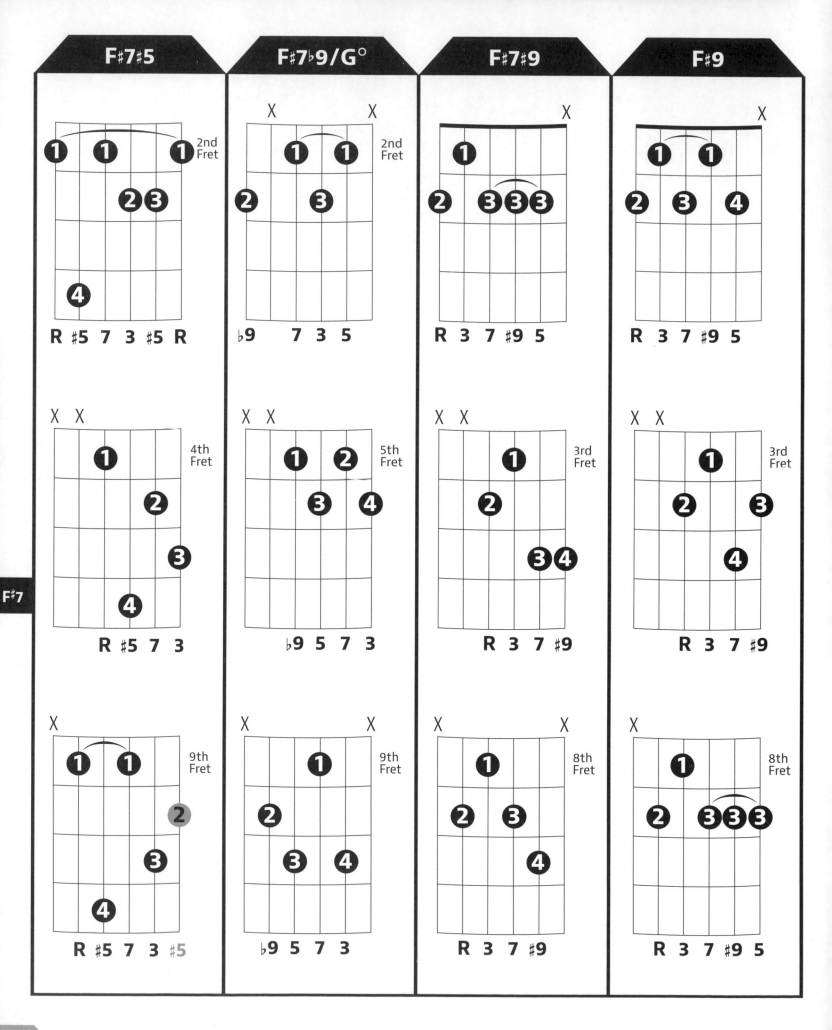

F♯7♯5

R ♯5 7 3 ♯5 R

R ♯5 7 3

R ♯5 7 3 ♯5

F♯7♭9/G°

♭9 7 3 5

♭9 5 7 3

♭9 5 7 3

F♯7♯9

R 3 7 ♯9 5

R 3 7 ♯9

R 3 7 ♯9

F♯9

R 3 7 ♯9 5

R 3 7 ♯9

R 3 7 ♯9 5

F♯7

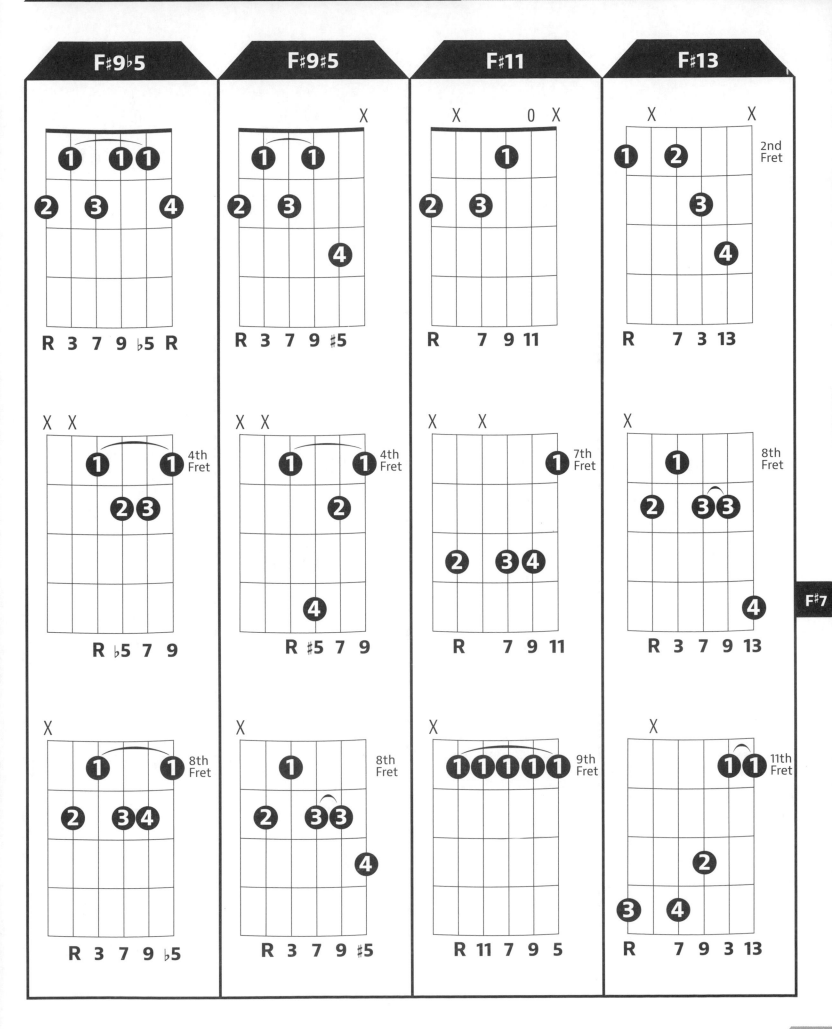

F#9♭5

R 3 7 9 ♭5 R

R ♭5 7 9

R 3 7 9 ♭5

F#9#5

R 3 7 9 #5

R #5 7 9

R 3 7 9 #5

F#11

R 7 9 11

R 7 9 11

R 11 7 9 5

F#13

R 7 3 13

R 3 7 9 13

R 7 9 3 13

F#7

G Major

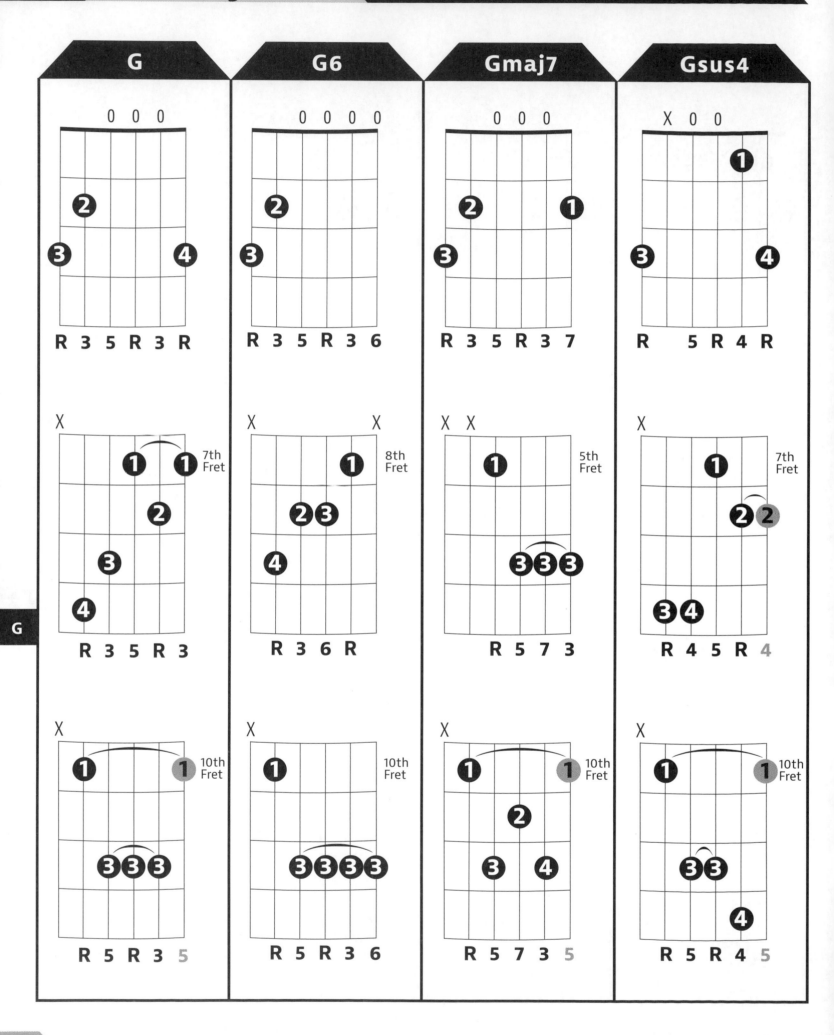

Minor   G

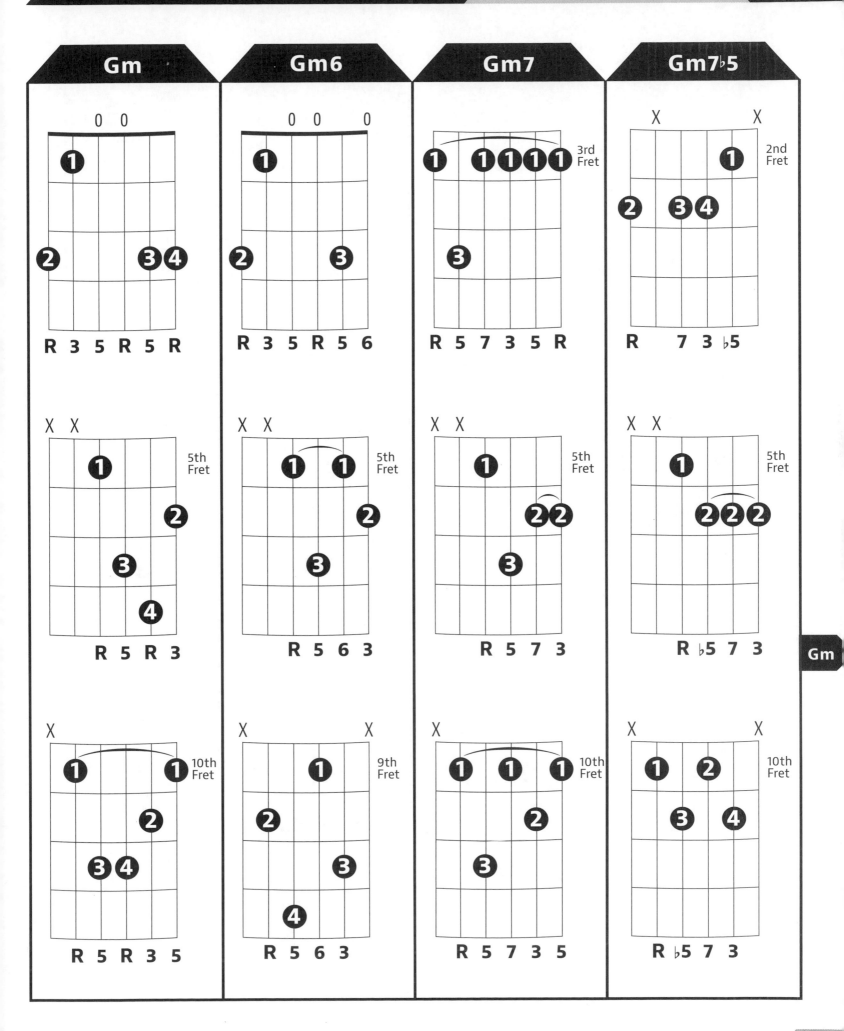

Gm | Gm6 | Gm7 | Gm7♭5

65

Gm

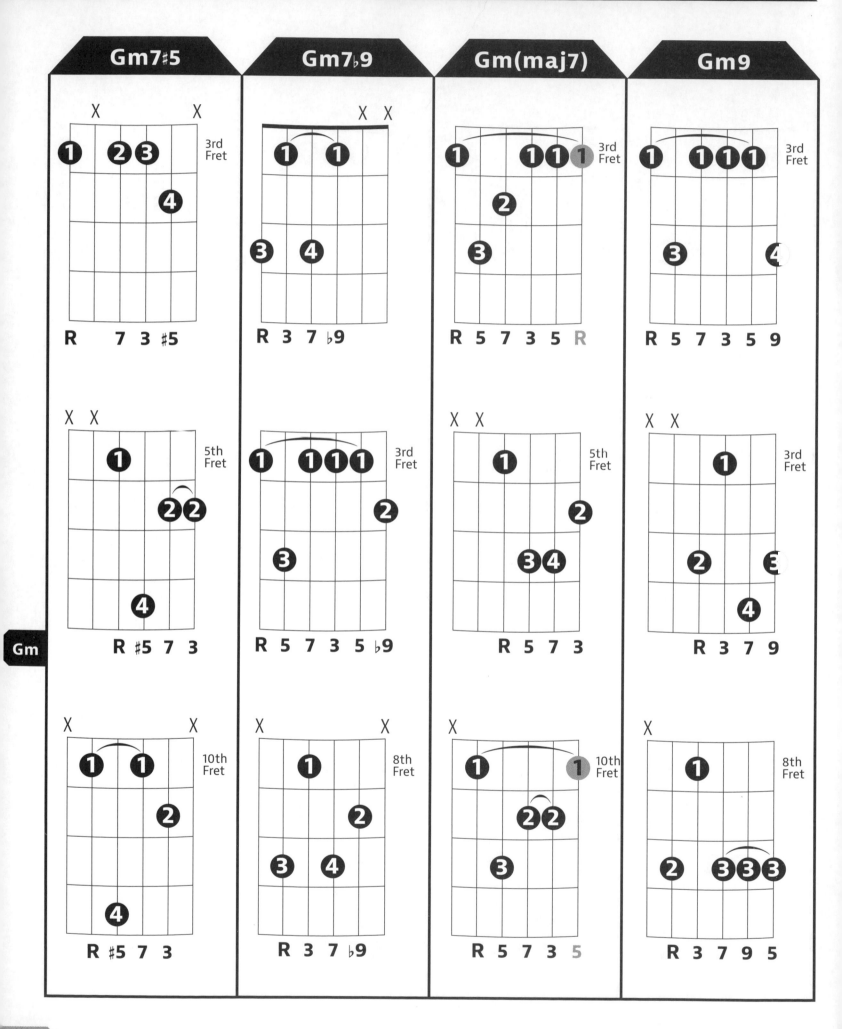

Gm7#5   Gm7♭9   Gm(maj7)   Gm9

Seventh

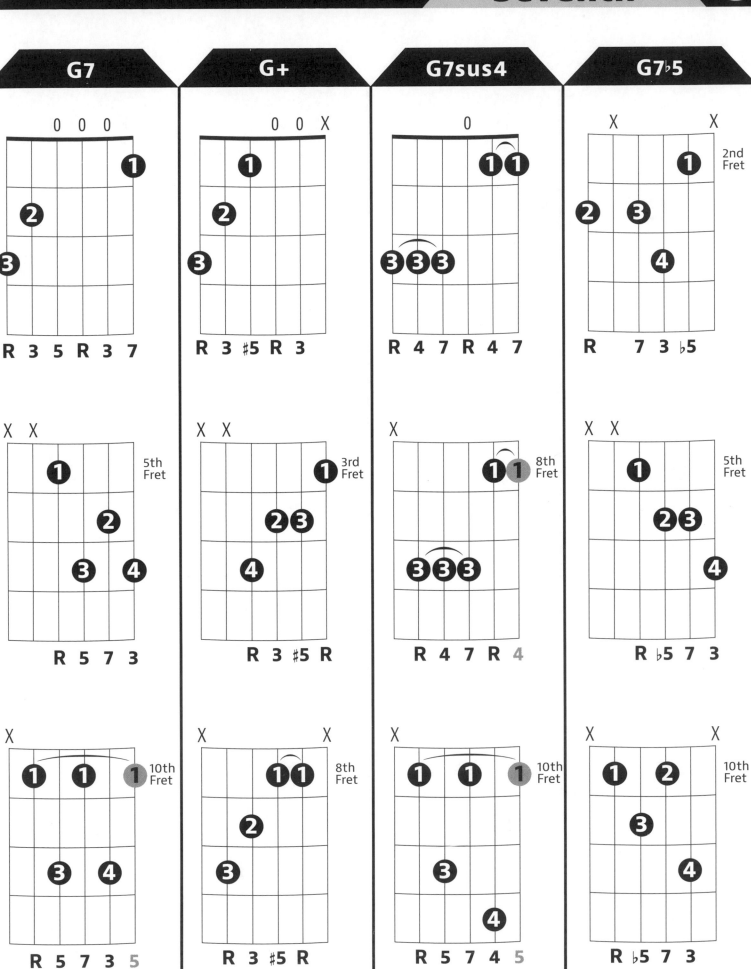

G7

G7#5

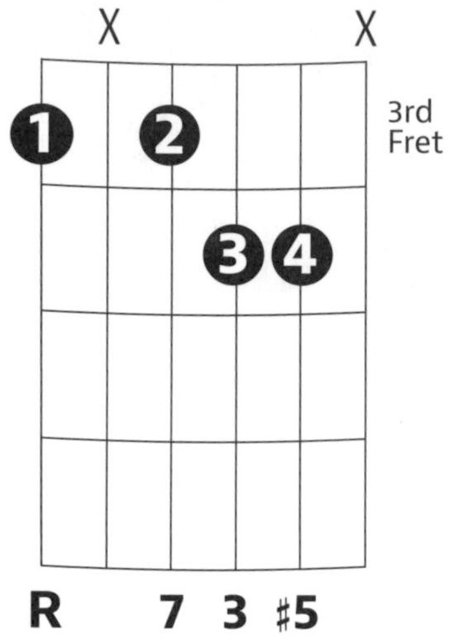

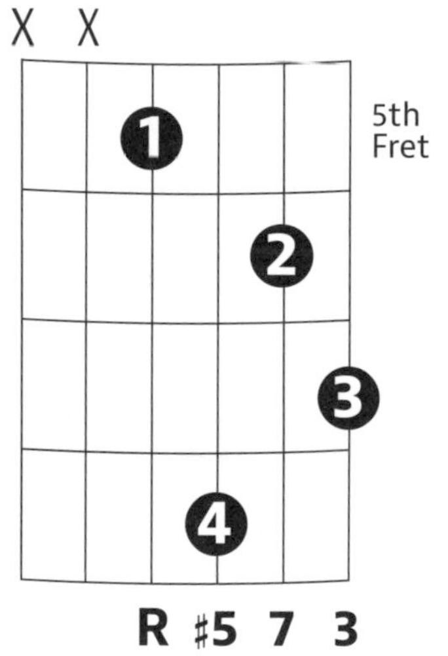

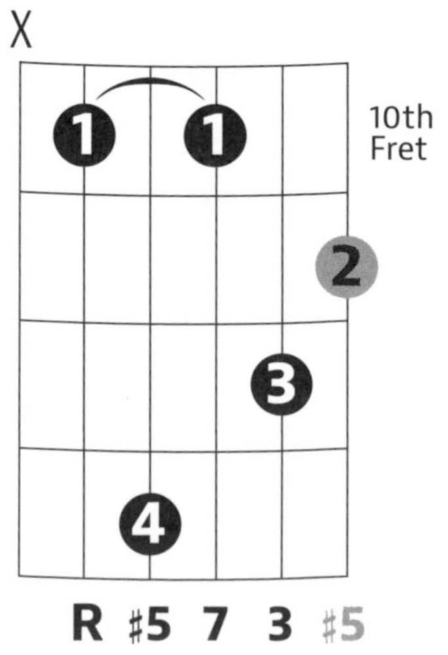

X   X

3rd Fret

R   7   3   #5

G7♭9/A♭°

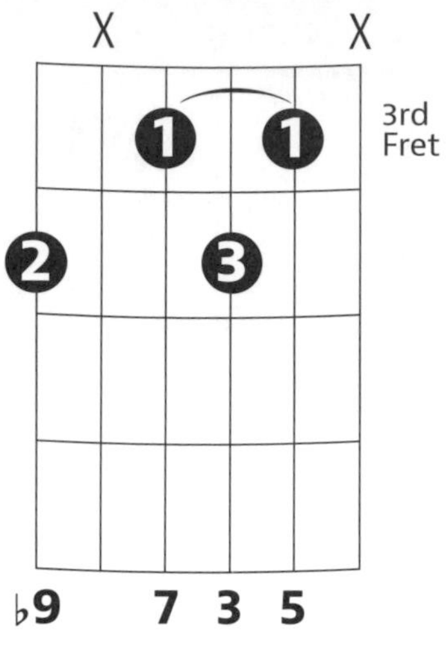

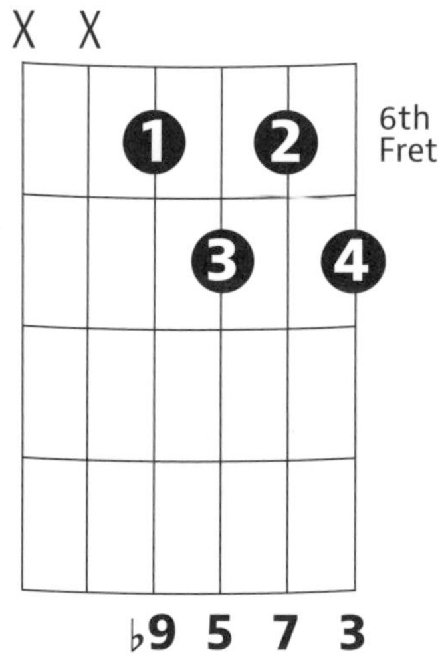

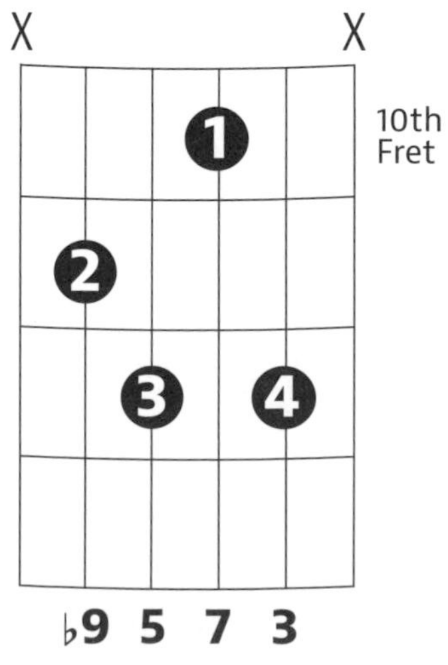

X   X

3rd Fret

♭9   7   3   5

G7#9

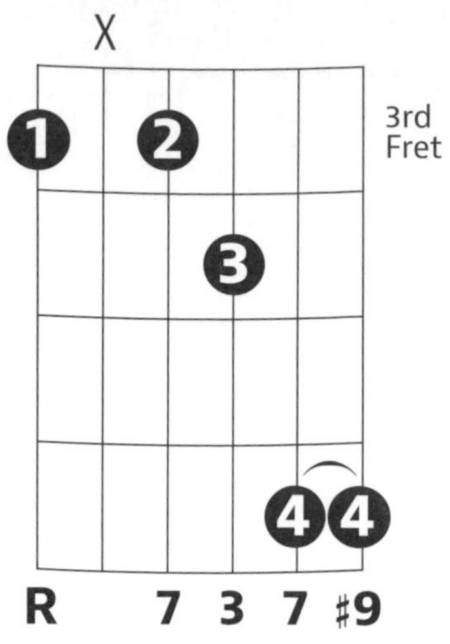

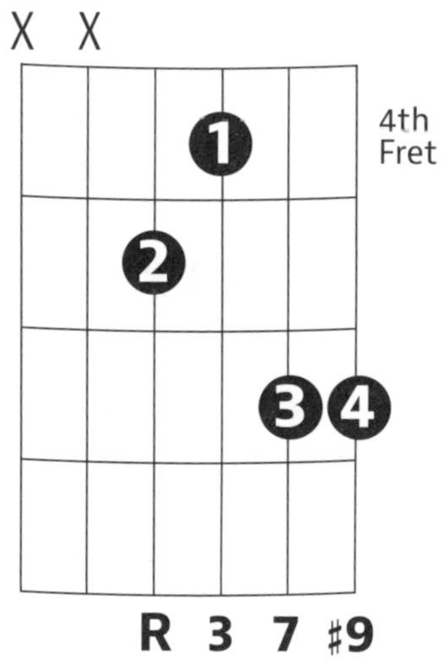

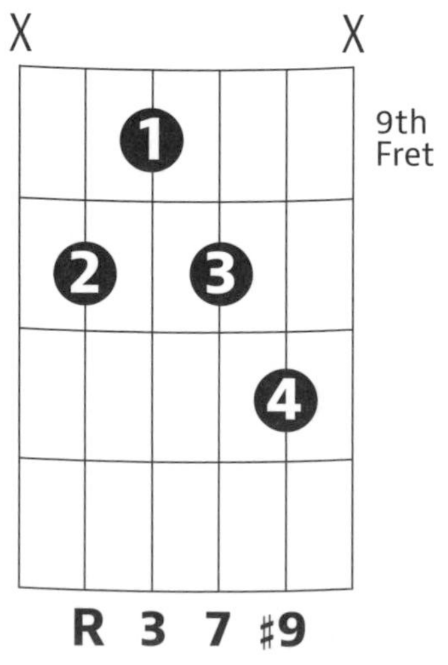

X

3rd Fret

R   7   3   7   #9

G9

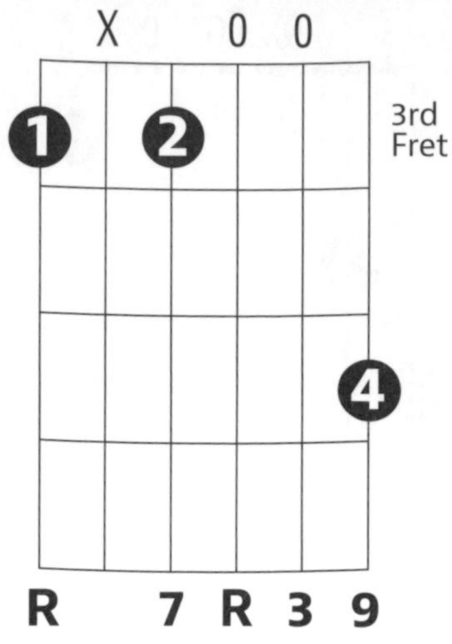

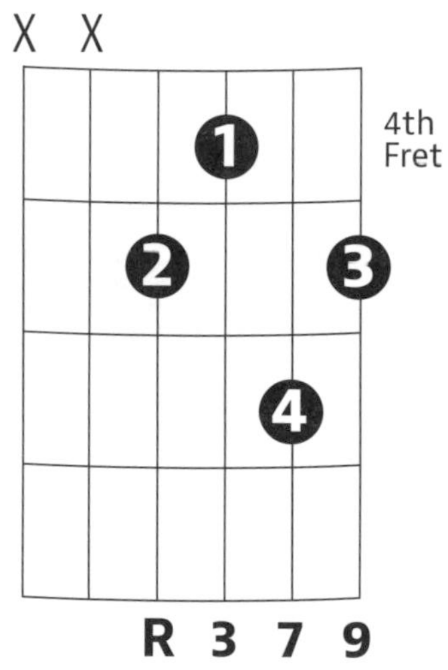

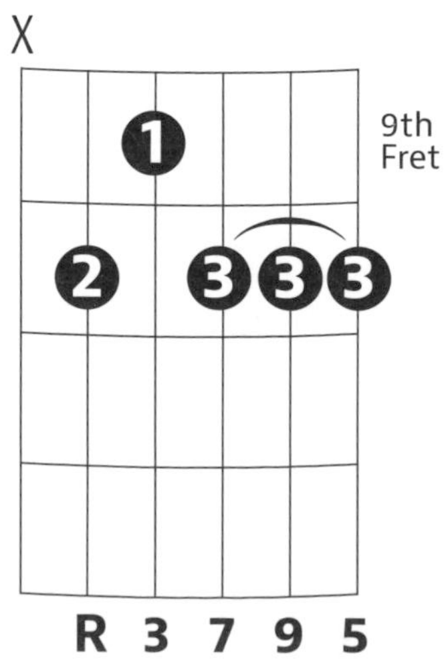

X   0   0

3rd Fret

R   7   R   3   9

X   X

5th Fret

R   #5   7   3

X   X

6th Fret

♭9   5   7   3

X   X

4th Fret

R   3   7   #9

X   X

4th Fret

R   3   7   9

G7

X

10th Fret

R   #5   7   3   #5

X   X

10th Fret

♭9   5   7   3

X   X

9th Fret

R   3   7   #9

X

9th Fret

R   3   7   9   5

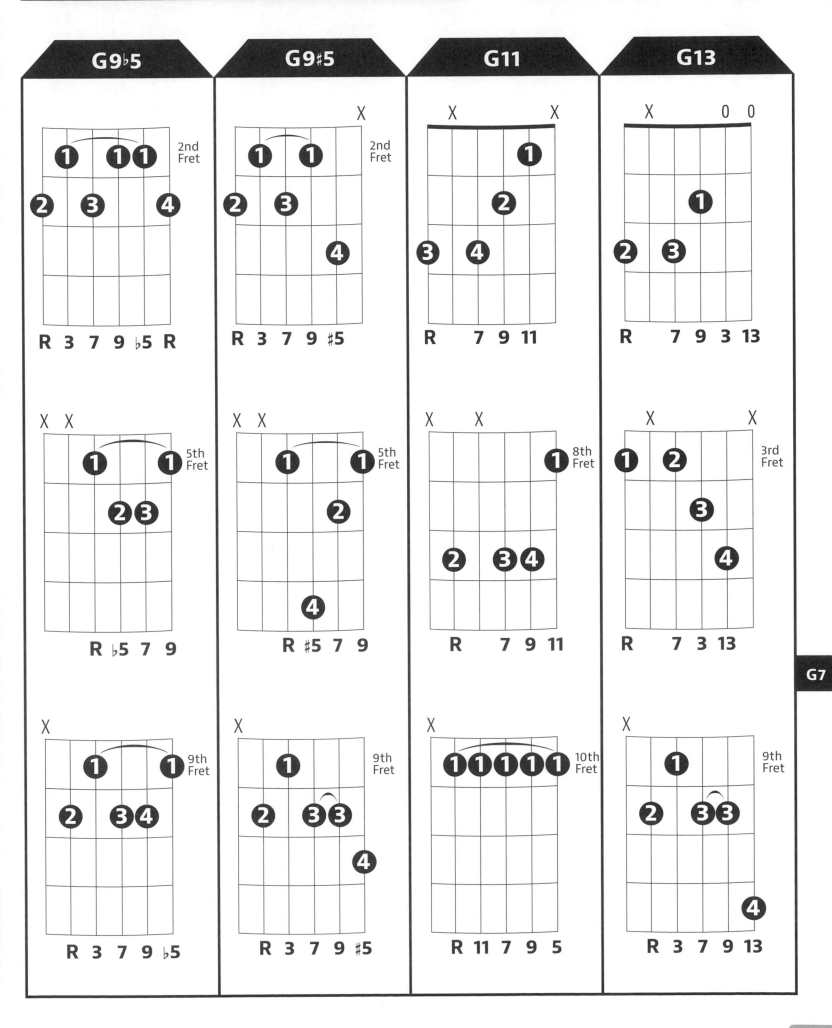

A♭/G♯ Major

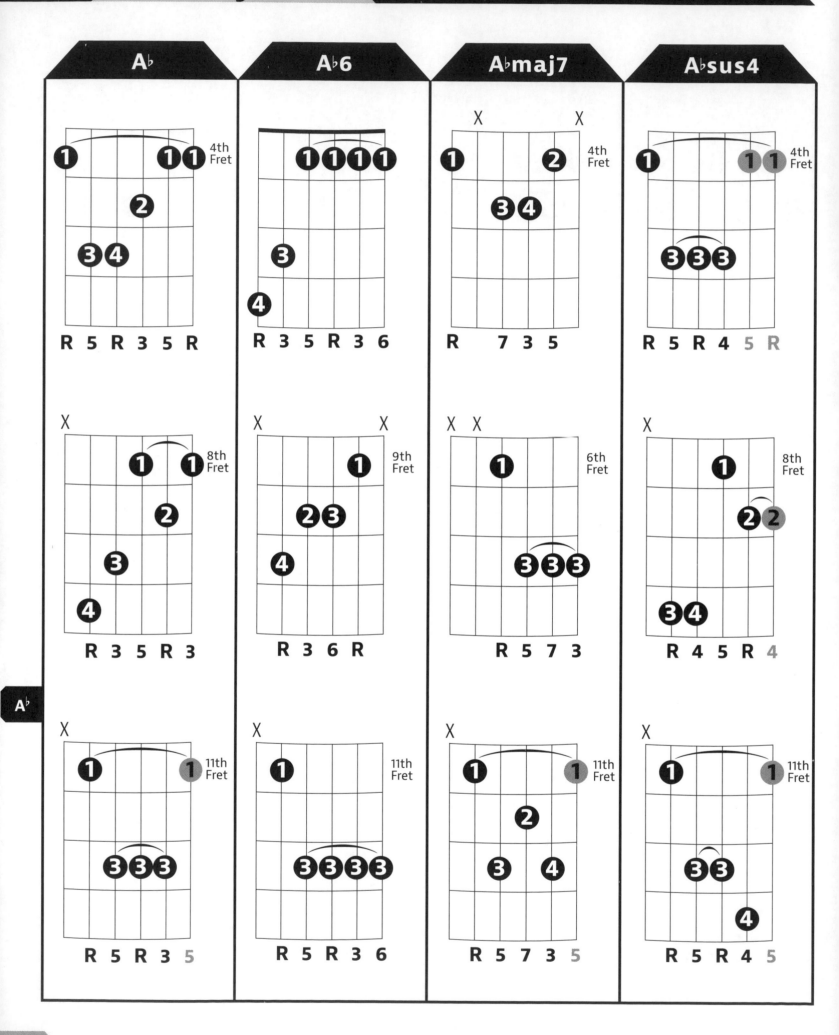

A♭
4th Fret
R 5 R 3 5 R

A♭6
R 3 5 R 3 6

A♭maj7
4th Fret
R 7 3 5

A♭sus4
4th Fret
R 5 R 4 5 R

8th Fret
R 3 5 R 3

9th Fret
R 3 6 R

6th Fret
R 5 7 3

8th Fret
R 4 5 R 4

11th Fret
R 5 R 3 5

11th Fret
R 5 R 3 6

11th Fret
R 5 7 3 5

11th Fret
R 5 R 4 5

Minor

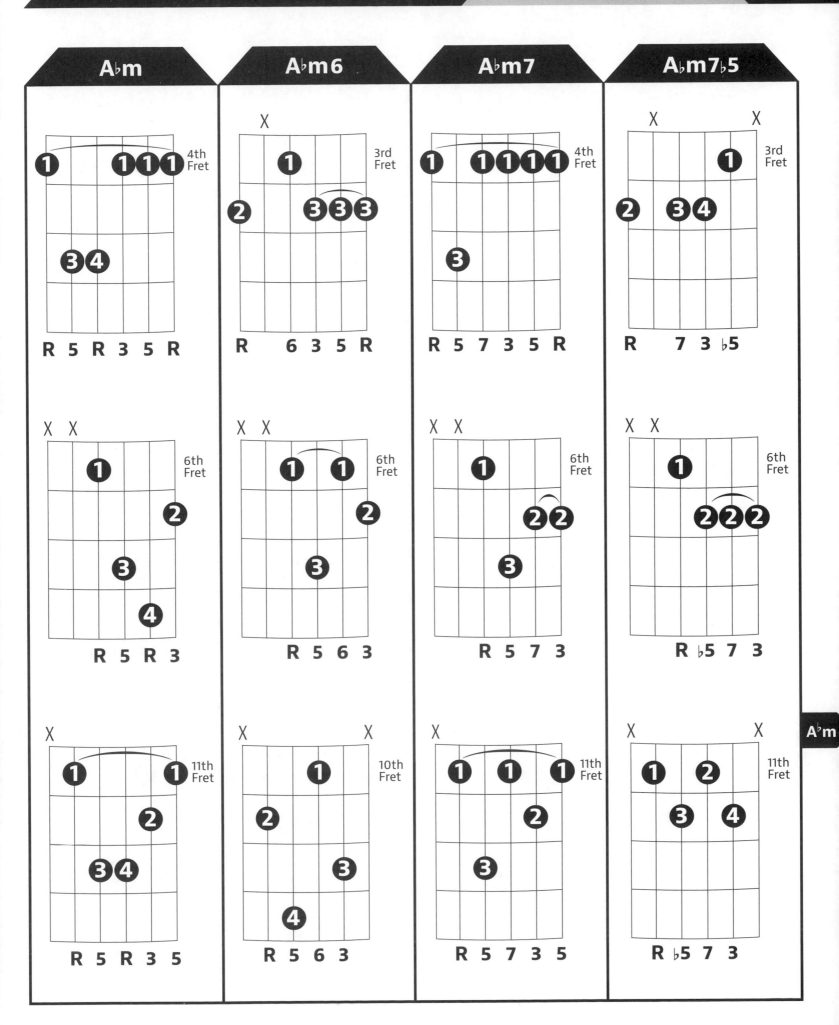

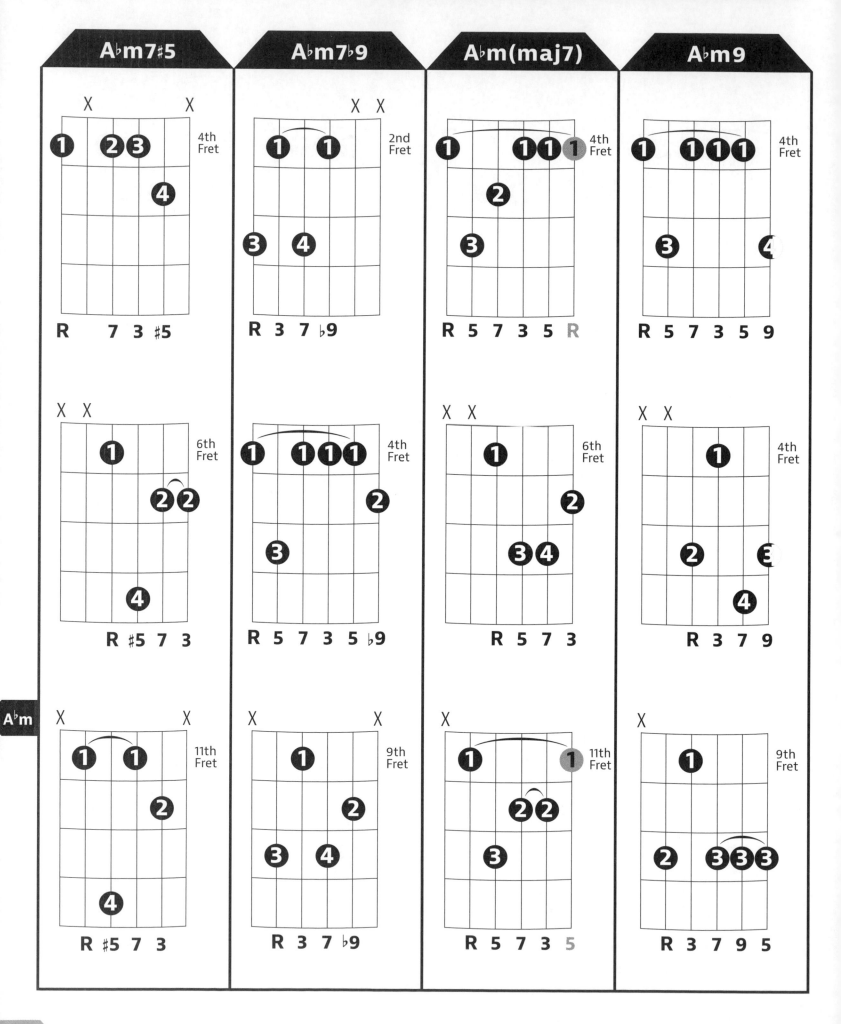

A♭m7♯5

A♭m7♭9

A♭m(maj7)

A♭m9

A♭m

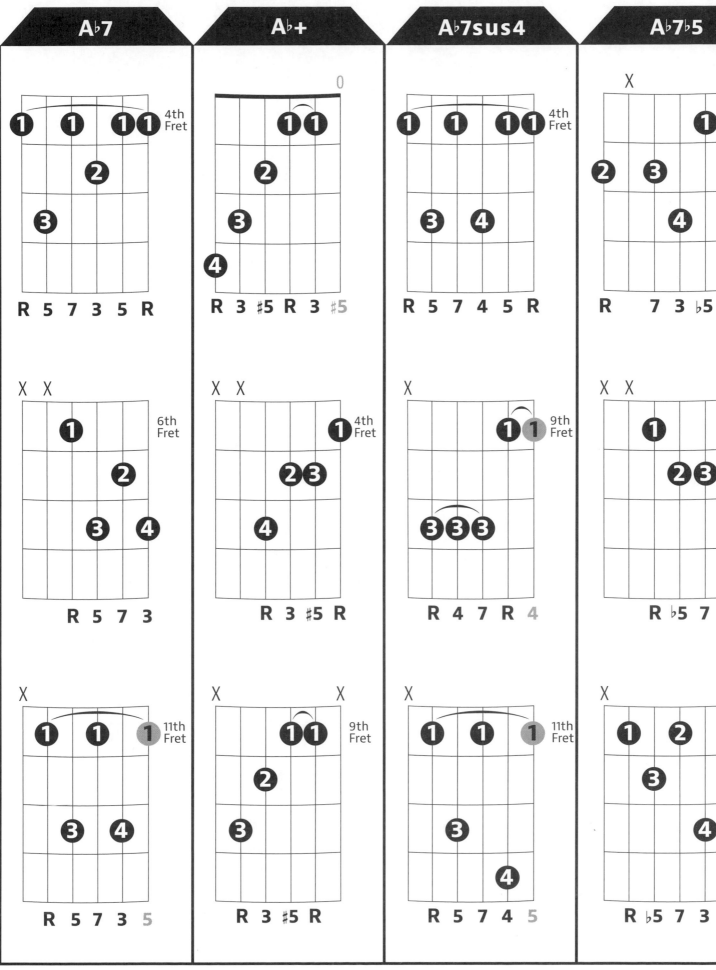

A♭7♯5

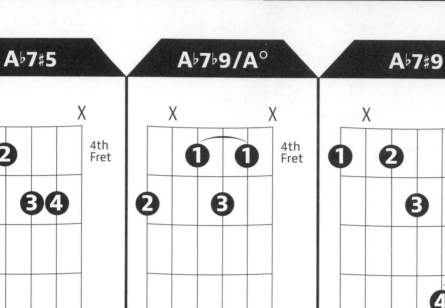

X   X

4th Fret

① **②**

③④

R 7 3 ♯5

X X

6th Fret

①

②

③

④

R ♯5 7 3

A♭7

X

11th Fret

① **①**

②

③

④

R ♯5 7 3 ♯5

A♭7♭9/A°

X   X

4th Fret

① **①**

② **③**

♭9 7 3 5

X X

7th Fret

① **②**

③ **④**

♭9 5 7 3

X   X

11th Fret

①

②

③ **④**

♭9 5 7 3

A♭7♯9

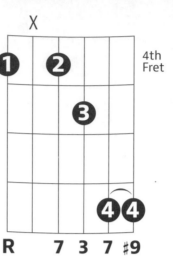

X

4th Fret

① **②**

③

④④

R 7 3 7 ♯9

X X

5th Fret

①

②

③④

R 3 7 ♯9

X   X

10th Fret

①

② **③**

④

R 3 7 ♯9

A♭9

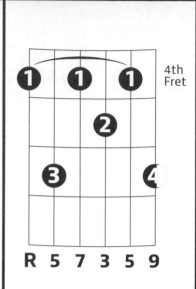

X

4th Fret

① **①** **①**

②

③   **④**

R 5 7 3 5 9

X X

5th Fret

①

②   **③**

④

R 3 7 9

X

10th Fret

①

② **③③③**

R 3 7 9 5

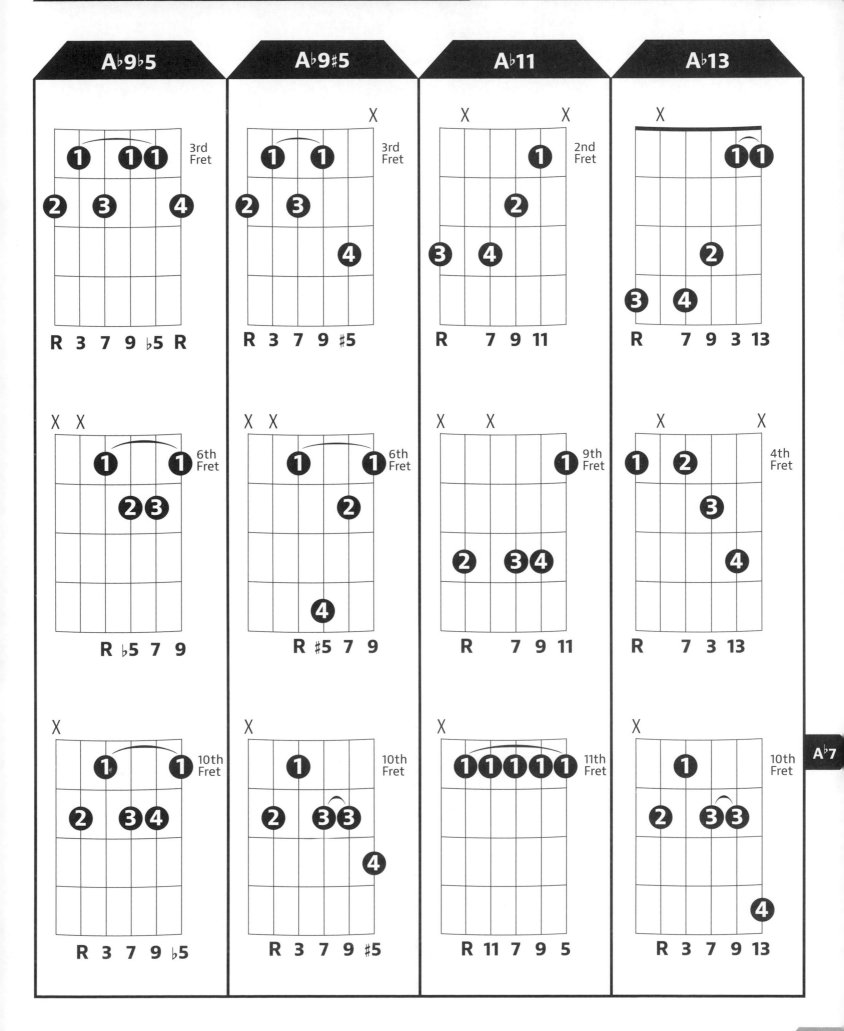

A♭9♭5   A♭9#5   A♭11   A♭13

A♭7

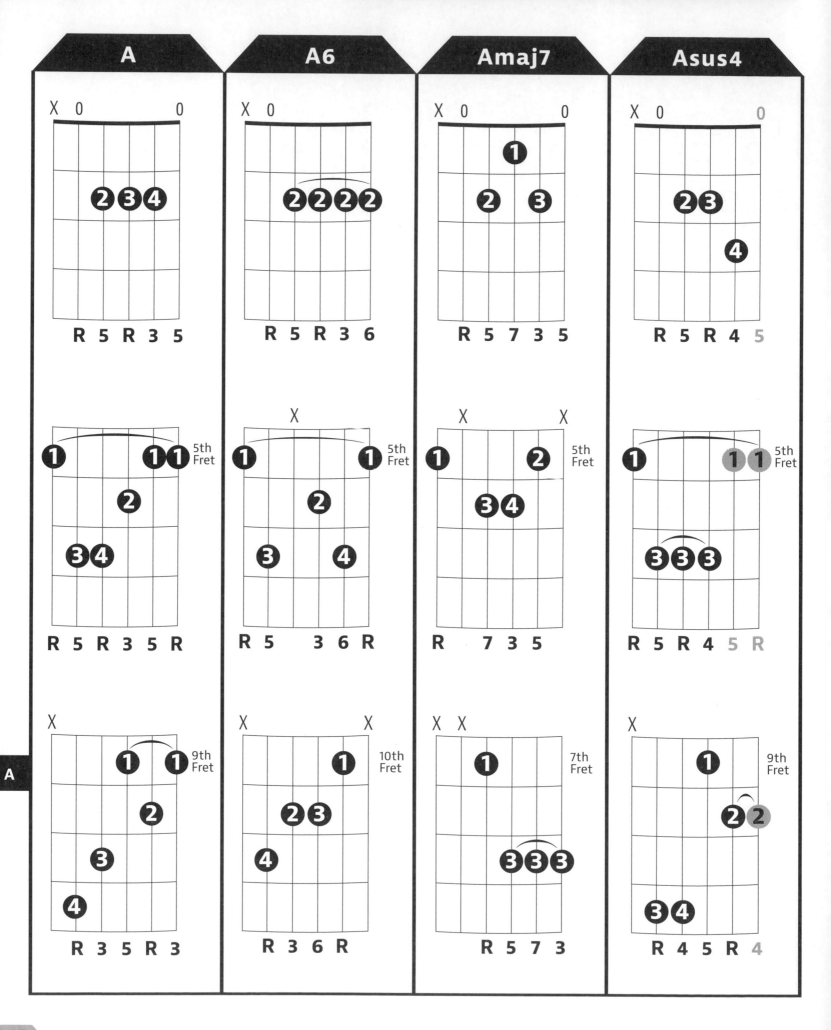

Minor

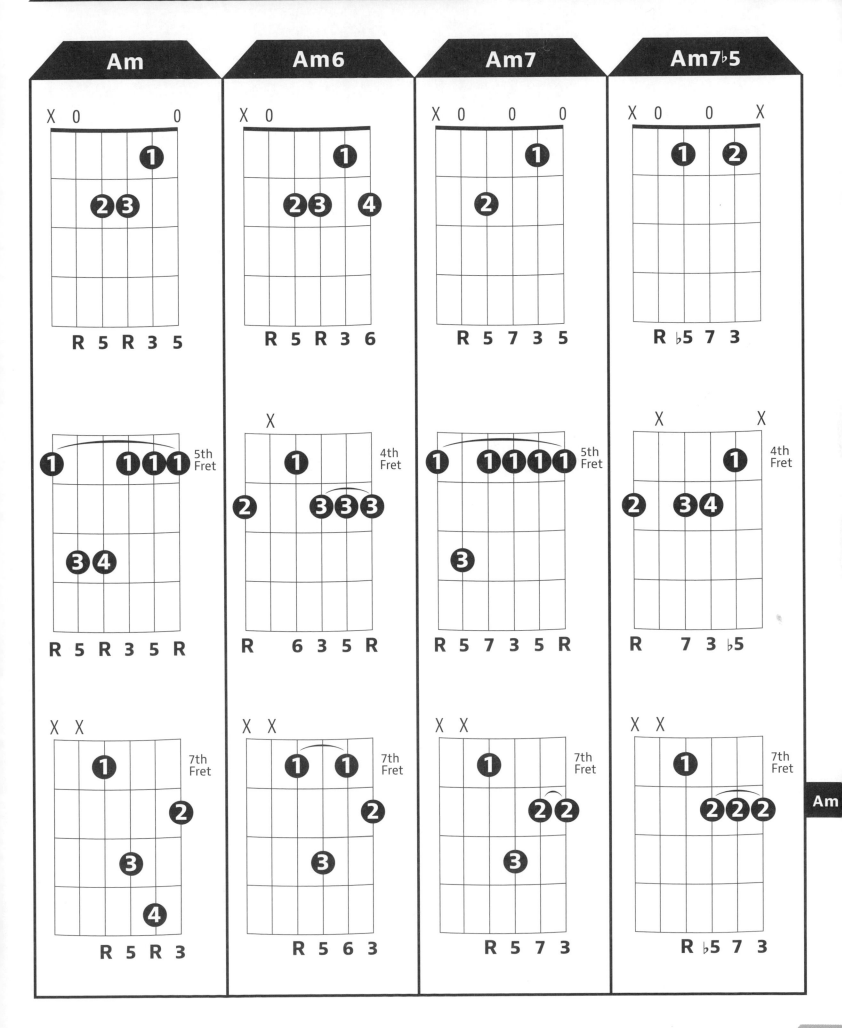

Am7#5

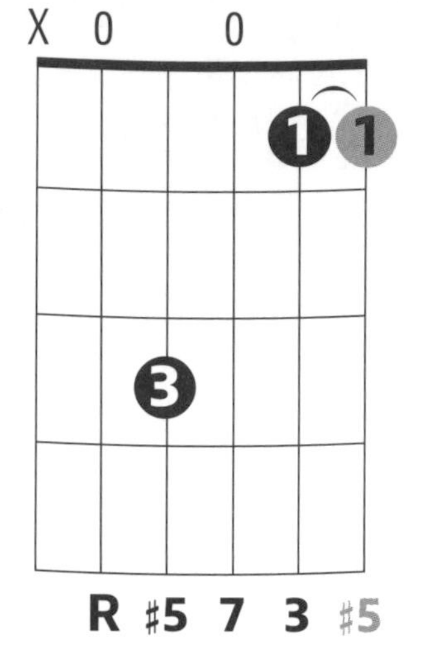

X 0 0

R #5 7 3 #5

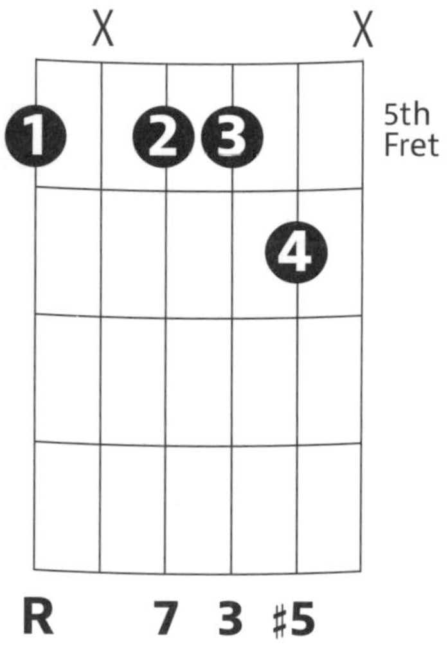

X X

5th Fret

R 7 3 #5

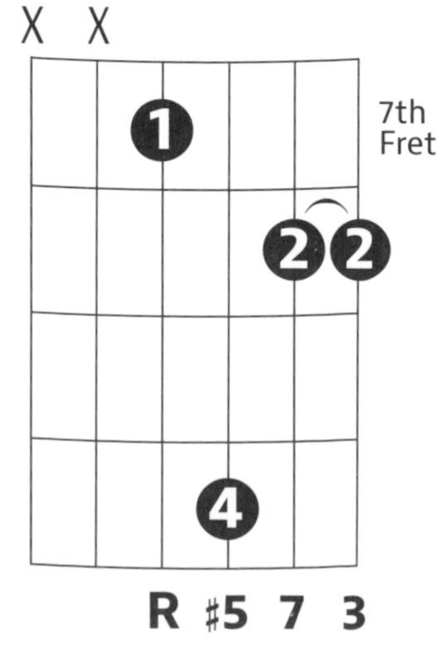

X X

7th Fret

R #5 7 3

Am7♭9

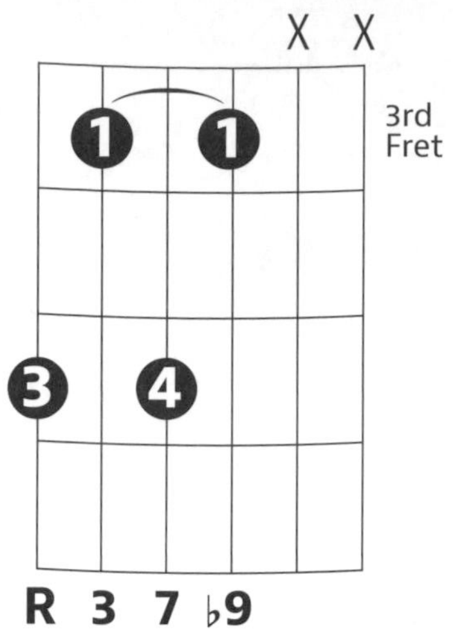

X X

3rd Fret

R 3 7 ♭9

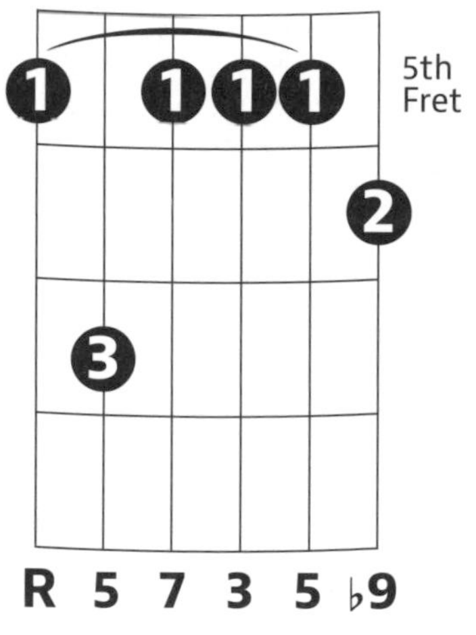

5th Fret

R 5 7 3 5 ♭9

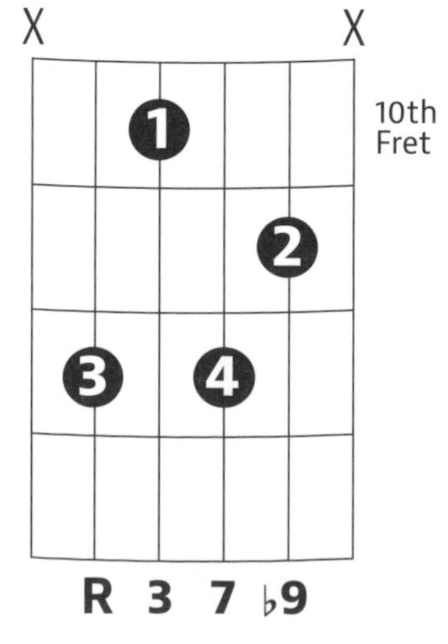

X X

10th Fret

R 3 7 ♭9

Am(maj7)

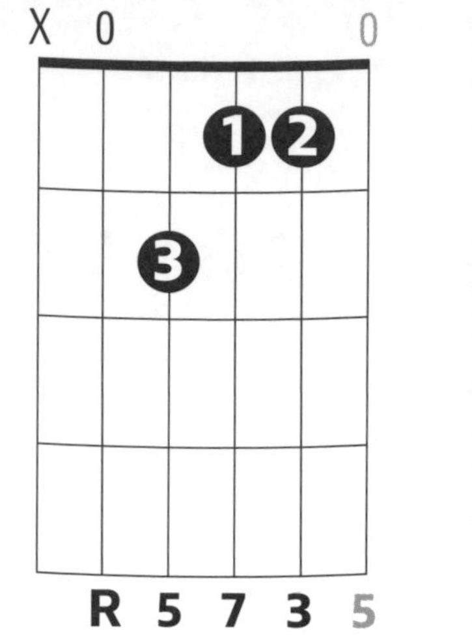

X 0 0

R 5 7 3 5

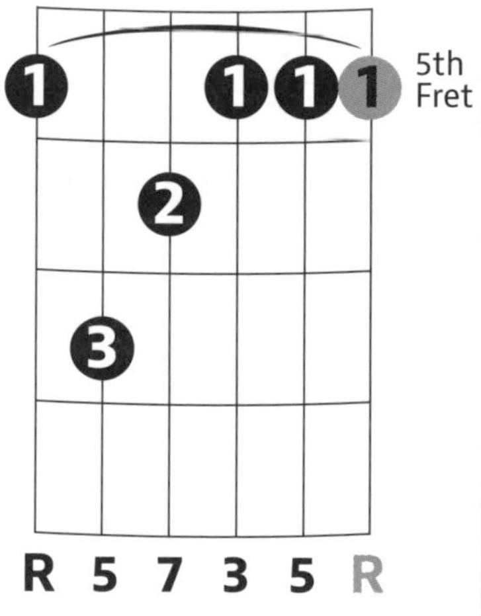

5th Fret

R 5 7 3 5 R

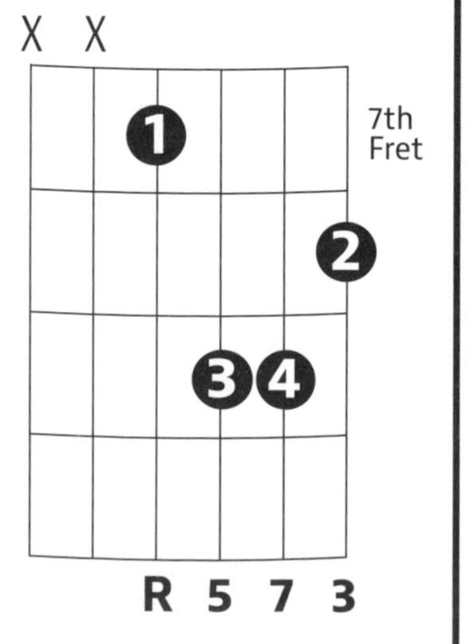

X X

7th Fret

R 5 7 3

Am9

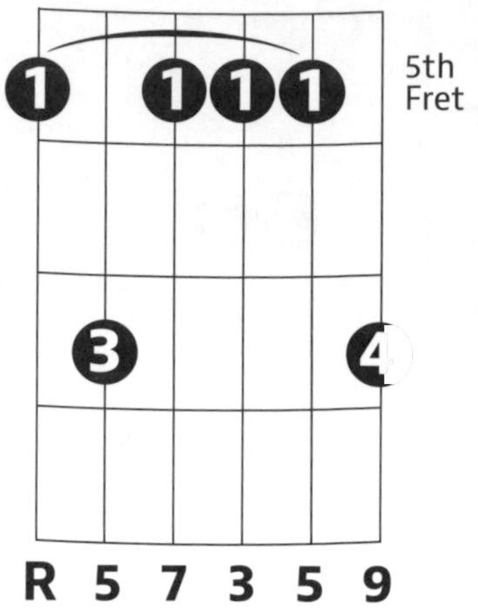

5th Fret

R 5 7 3 5 9

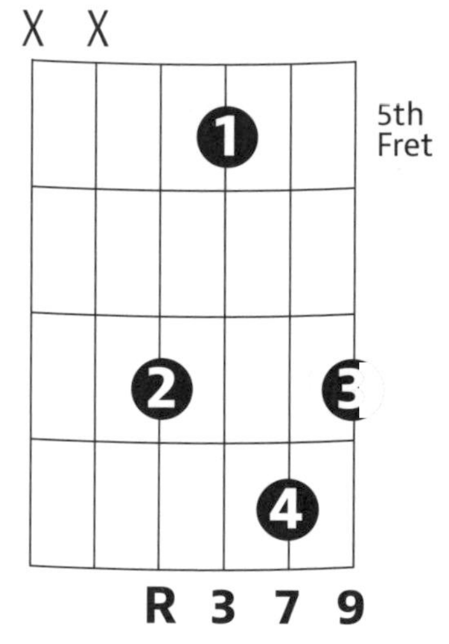

X X

5th Fret

R 3 7 9

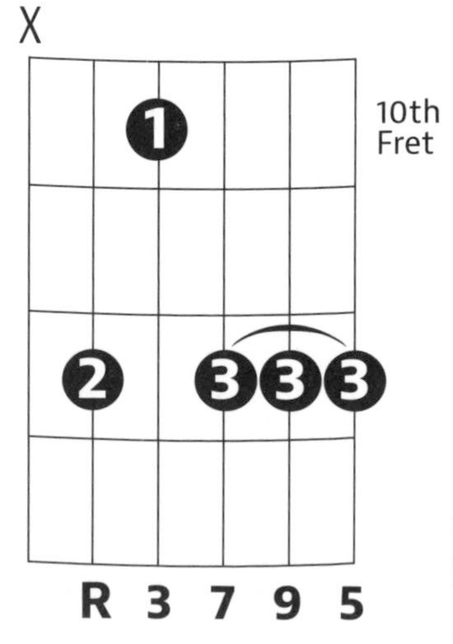

X

10th Fret

R 3 7 9 5

Am

A7

X 0 0 0

2 3

R 5 7 3 5

A+

X 0

1

3 2

4

R #5 R 3 #5

A7sus4

X 0 0 0

2

4

R 5 7 4 5

A7♭5

X 0 0 X

2

3

R ♭5 7 3

A7 (second position)

1 1 1 1 — 5th Fret

2

3

R 5 7 3 5 R

A+ (second position)

X

1 1

2

3

4

R 3 #5 R 3

A7sus4 (second position)

1 1 1 1 1 — 5th Fret

3 4

R 5 7 4 5 R

A7♭5 (second position)

X X

1 — 4th Fret

2 3

4

R 7 3 ♭5

A7 (third position)

X X

1 — 7th Fret

2

3 4

R 5 7 3

A+ (third position)

X X

1 — 5th Fret

2 3

4

R 3 #5 R

A7sus4 (third position)

X

1 1 — 10th Fret

3 3 3

R 4 7 R 4

A7♭5 (third position)

X X

1 — 7th Fret

2 3

4

R ♭5 7 3

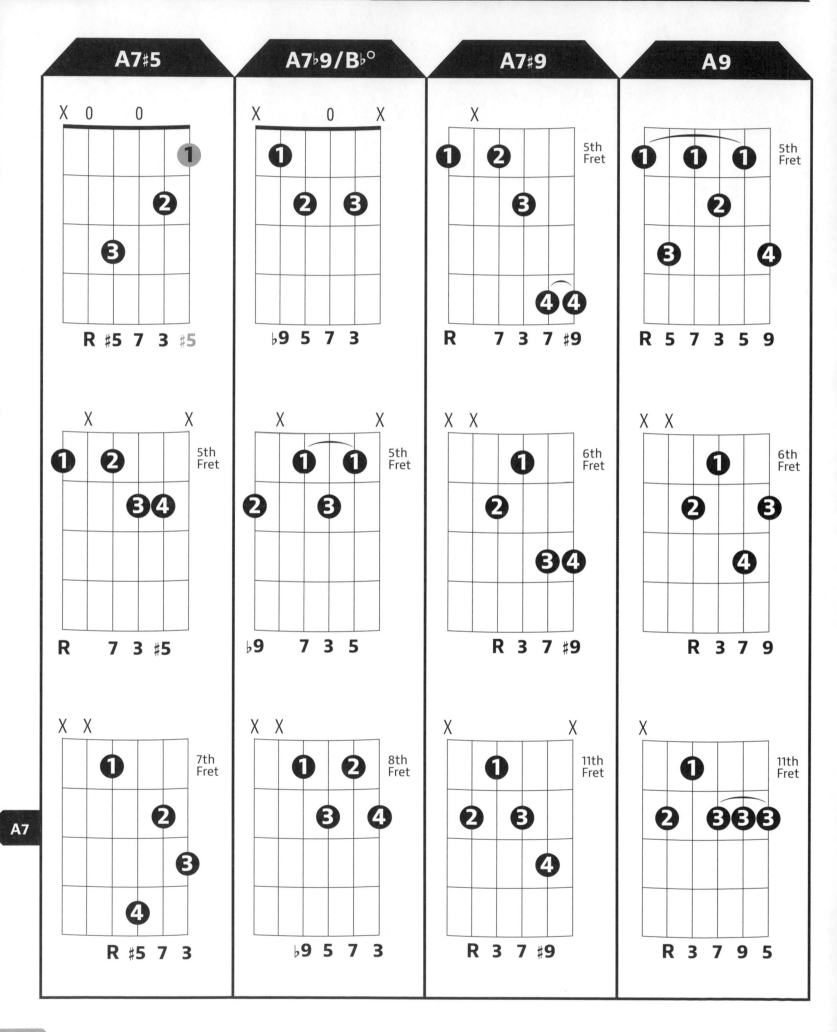

A7#5

X 0 0

R #5 7 3 #5

X X

5th Fret

R 7 3 #5

X X

7th Fret

R #5 7 3

A7♭9/B♭°

X 0 X

♭9 5 7 3

X X

5th Fret

♭9 7 3 5

X X

8th Fret

♭9 5 7 3

A7#9

X

5th Fret

R 7 3 7 #9

X X

6th Fret

R 3 7 #9

X X

11th Fret

R 3 7 #9

A9

5th Fret

R 5 7 3 5 9

X X

6th Fret

R 3 7 9

X

11th Fret

R 3 7 9 5

A7

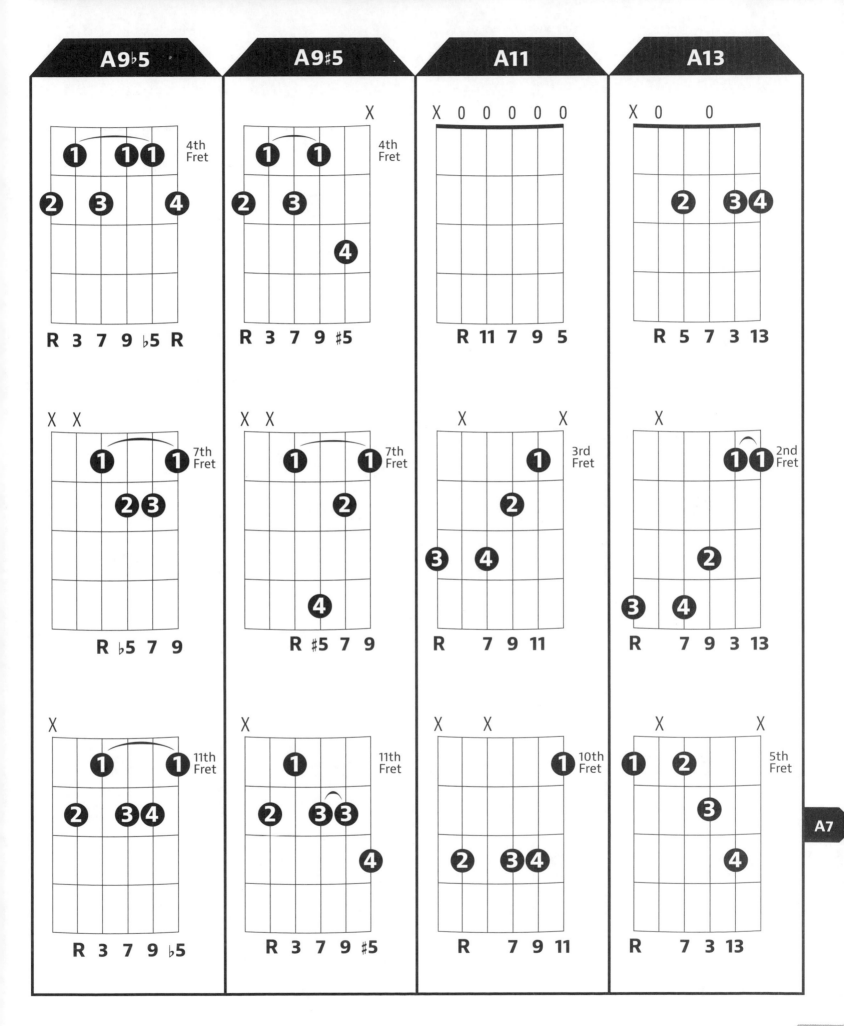

B♭/A♯   Major

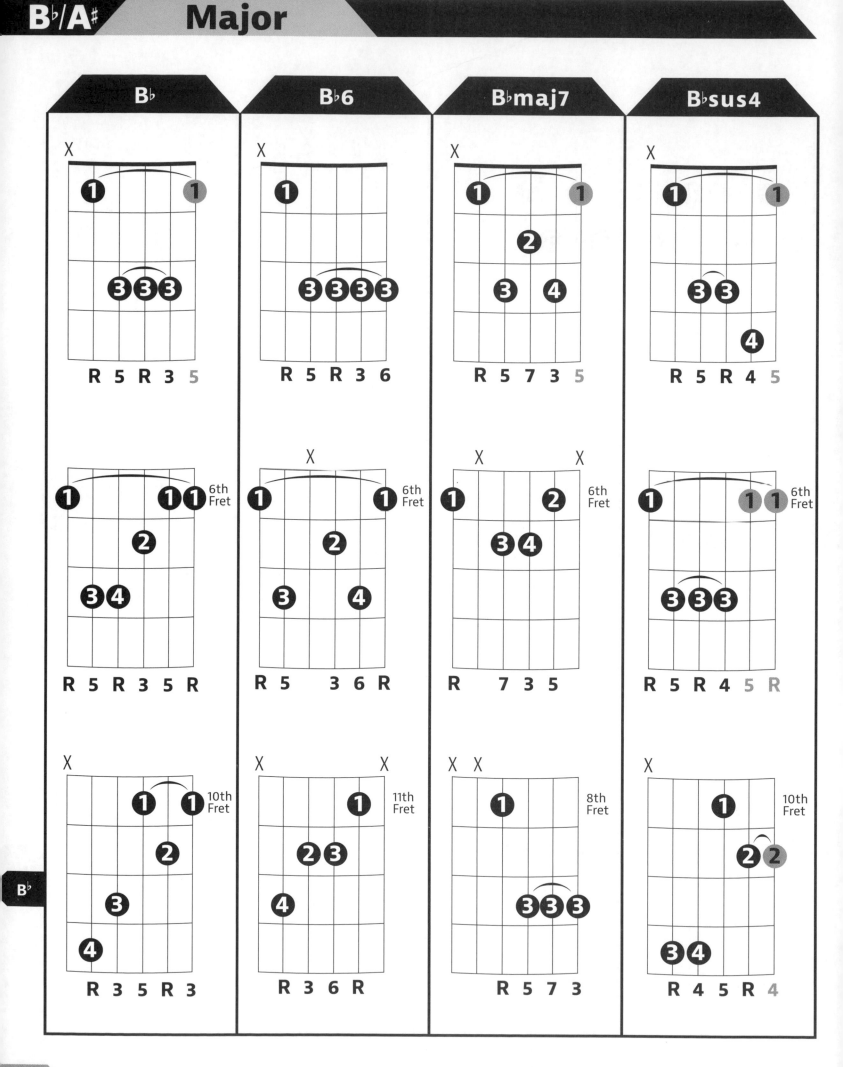

B♭

X

R 5 R 3 5

R 5 R 3 5 R

R 3 5 R 3

B♭6

X

R 5 R 3 6

R 5   3 6 R

R 3 6 R

B♭maj7

X

R 5 7 3 5

R   7 3 5

R 5 7 3

B♭sus4

X

R 5 R 4 5

R 5 R 4 5 R

R 4 5 R 4

6th Fret

6th Fret

6th Fret

6th Fret

10th Fret

11th Fret

8th Fret

10th Fret

B♭

Minor

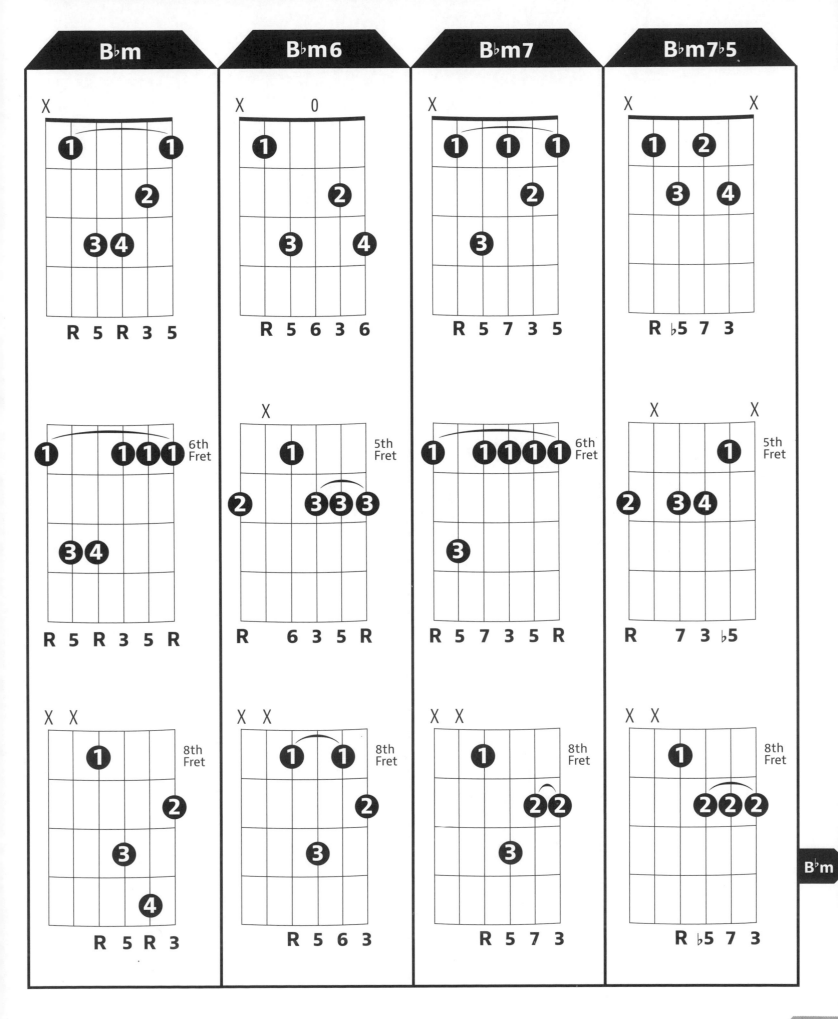

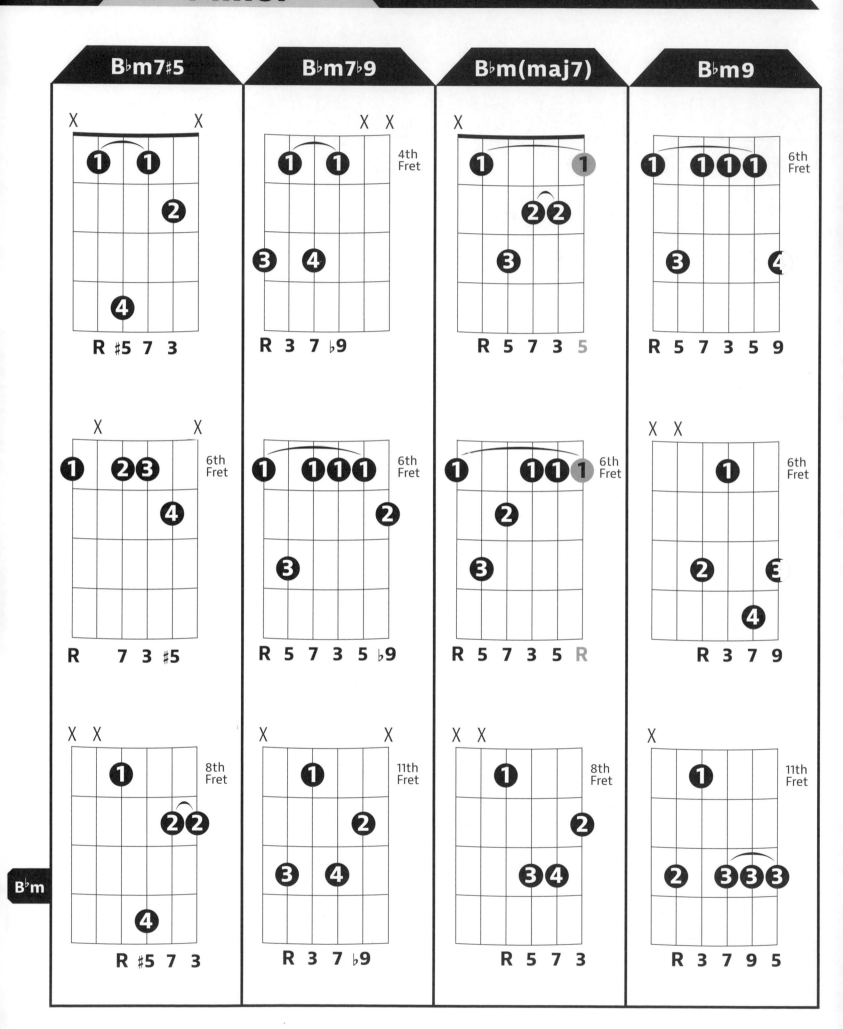

B♭m7#5

X   X

| 1 | | 1 | |
| 2 |
| 4 |

R #5 7 3

B♭m7♭9

X X

4th Fret

| 1 | | 1 |
| 3 | | 4 |

R 3 7 ♭9

B♭m(maj7)

X

| 1 | | | 1 |
| 2 2 |
| 3 |

R 5 7 3 5

B♭m9

6th Fret

| 1 | 1 | 1 | 1 |
| 3 | | 4 |

R 5 7 3 5 9

X   X

6th Fret

| 1 | | 2 | 3 |
| 4 |

R   7 3 #5

X   X

6th Fret

| 1 | 1 | 1 | 1 |
| 2 |
| 3 |

R 5 7 3 5 ♭9

X

6th Fret

| 1 | | 1 | 1 | 1 |
| 2 |
| 3 |

R 5 7 3 5 R

X X

6th Fret

| 1 |
| 2 | | 3 |
| 4 |

R 3 7 9

X X

8th Fret

| 1 |
| 2 2 |
| 4 |

R #5 7 3

X   X

11th Fret

| 1 |
| 2 |
| 3 | | 4 |

R 3 7 ♭9

X X

8th Fret

| 1 |
| 2 |
| 3 4 |

R 5 7 3

X

11th Fret

| 1 |
| 2 |
| 2 | | 3 3 3 |

R 3 7 9 5

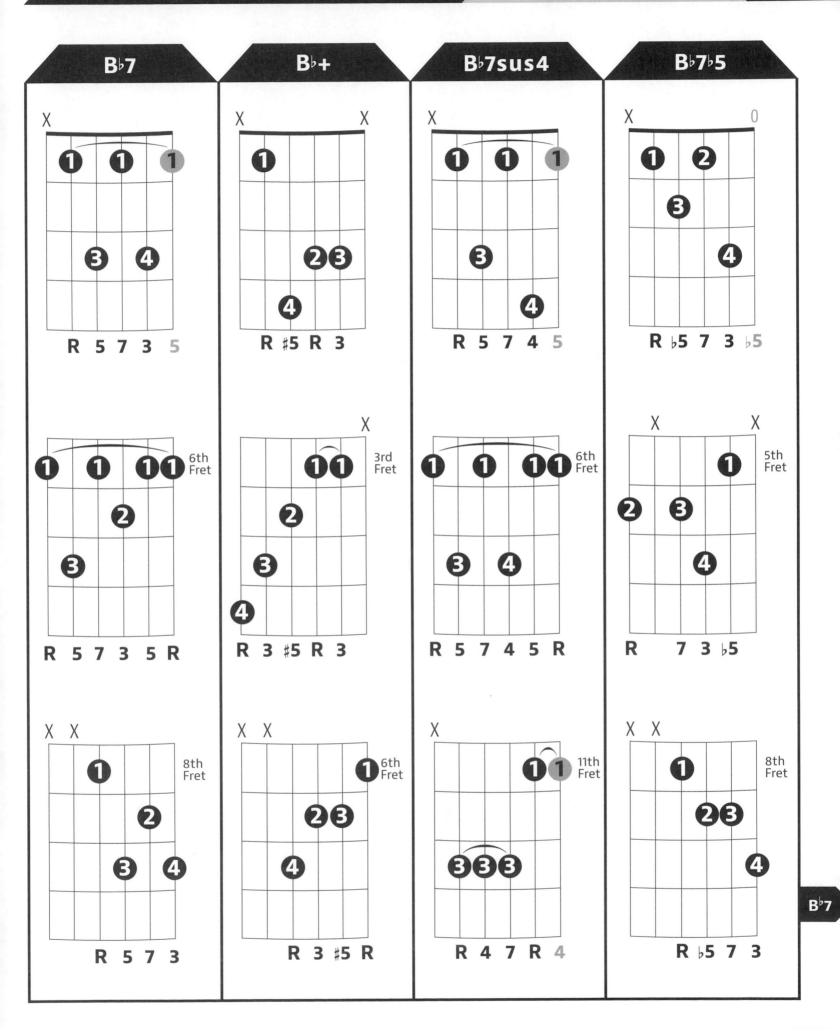

B♭7#5

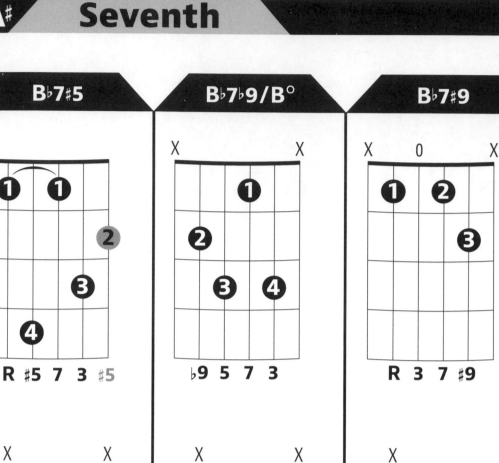

R #5 7 3 #5

B♭7♭9/B°

♭9 5 7 3

B♭7#9

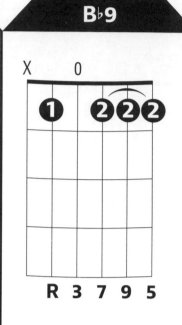

R 3 7 #9

B♭9

R 3 7 9 5

X   X

6th Fret

R   7 3 #5

X   X

6th Fret

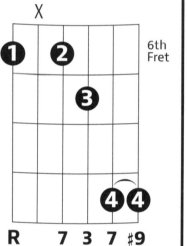

♭9   7 3 5

X

6th Fret

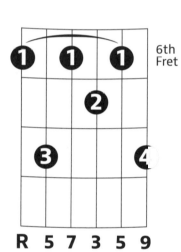

R   7 3 7 #9

6th Fret

R 5 7 3 5 9

X   X

8th Fret

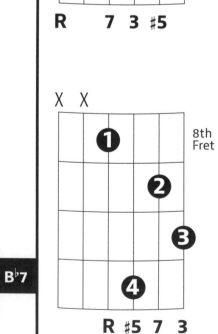

R #5 7 3

X   X

9th Fret

♭9 5 7 3

X   X

7th Fret

R 3 7 #9

X   X

7th Fret

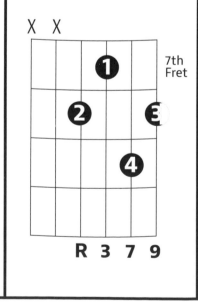

R 3 7 9

Seventh   B♭/A#

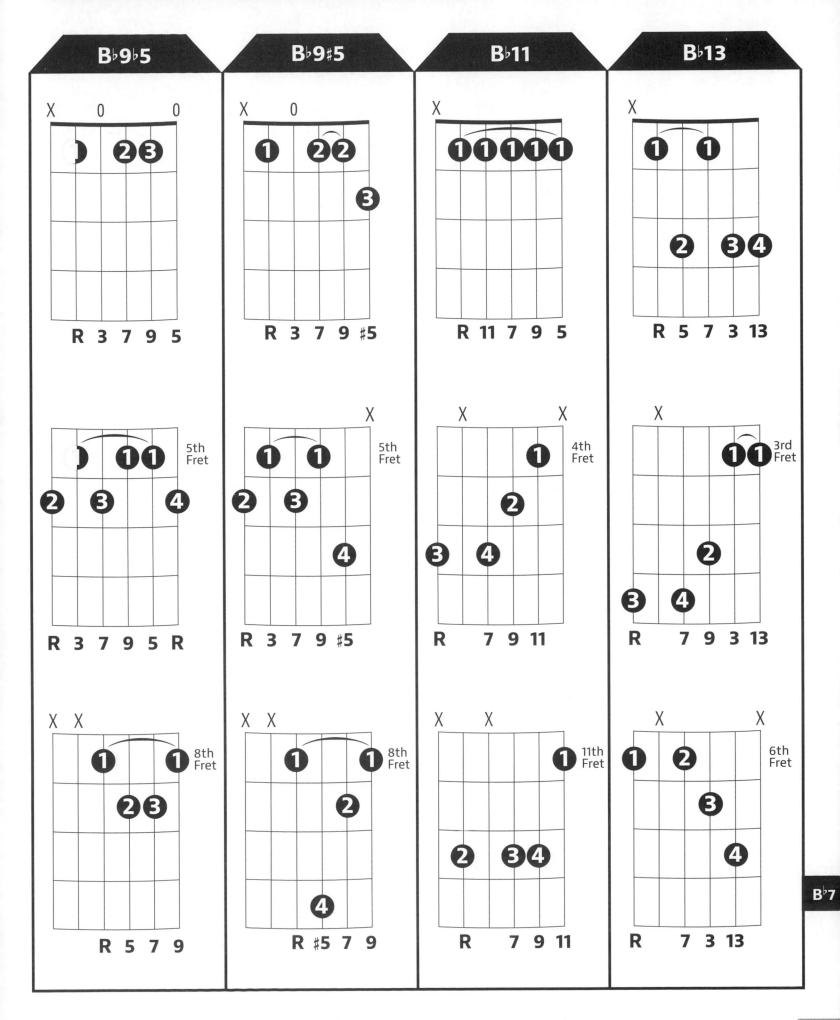

B Major

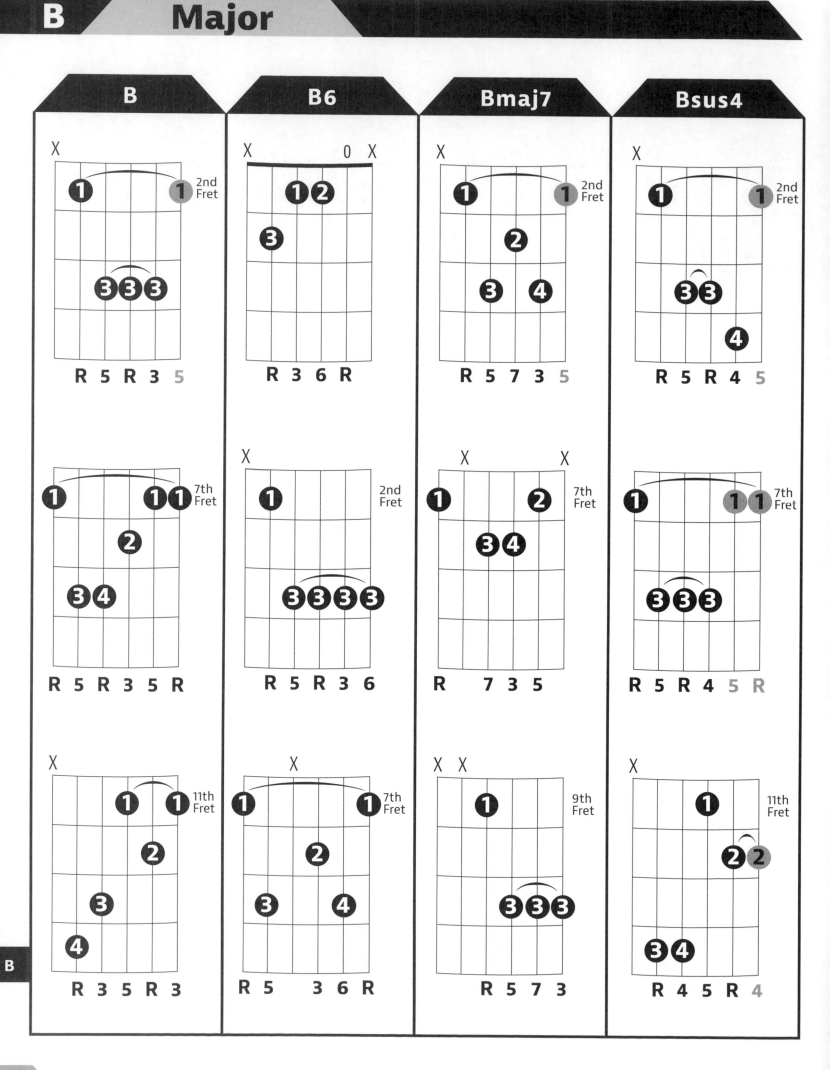

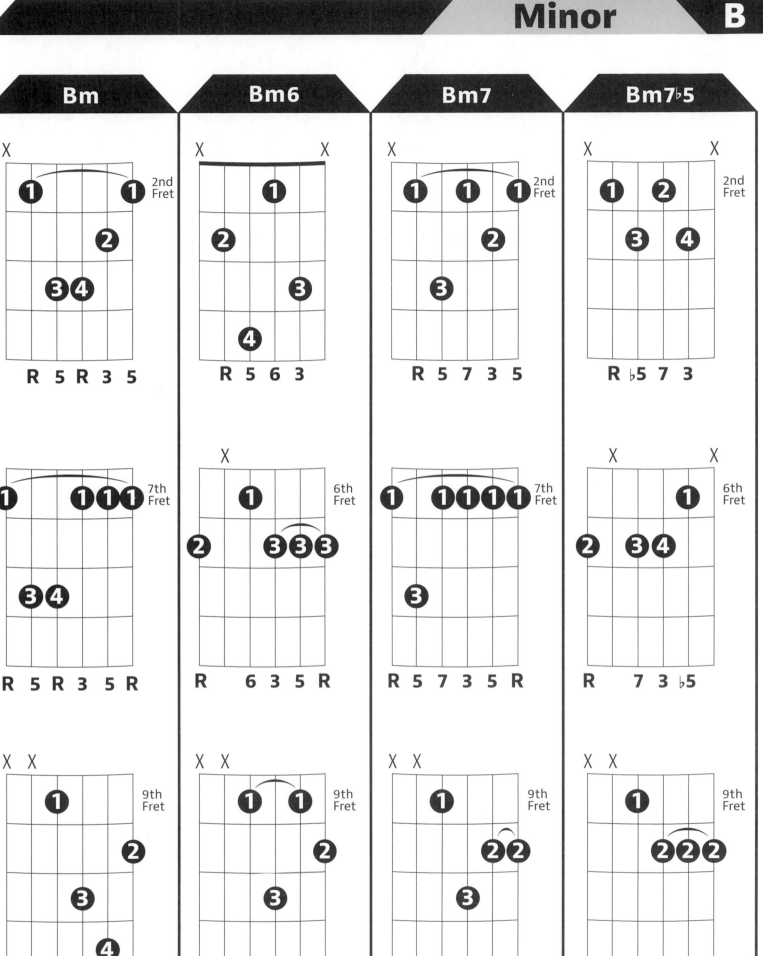

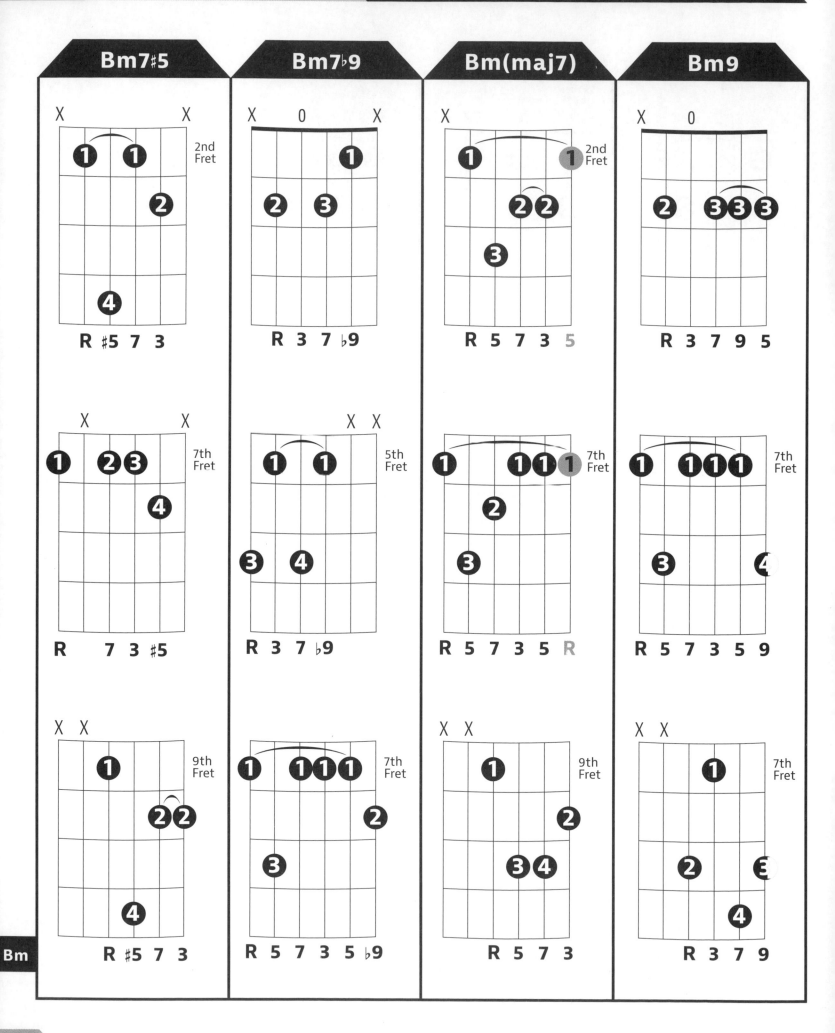

Bm7#5   Bm7♭9   Bm(maj7)   Bm9

Seventh   B

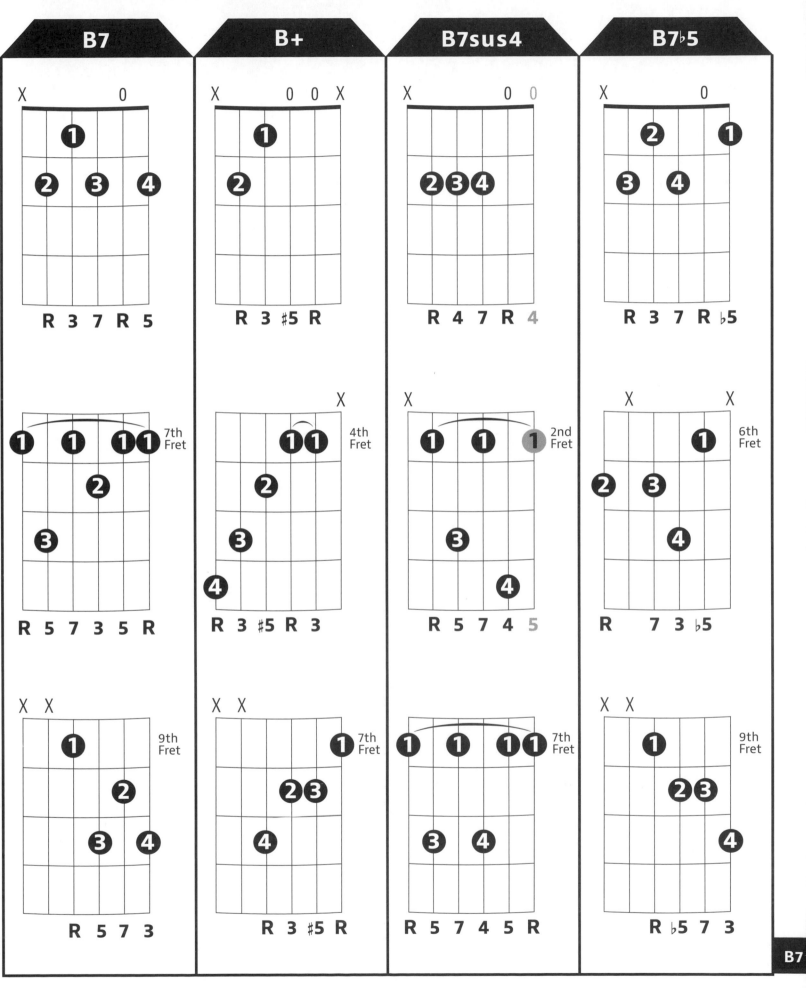

B7

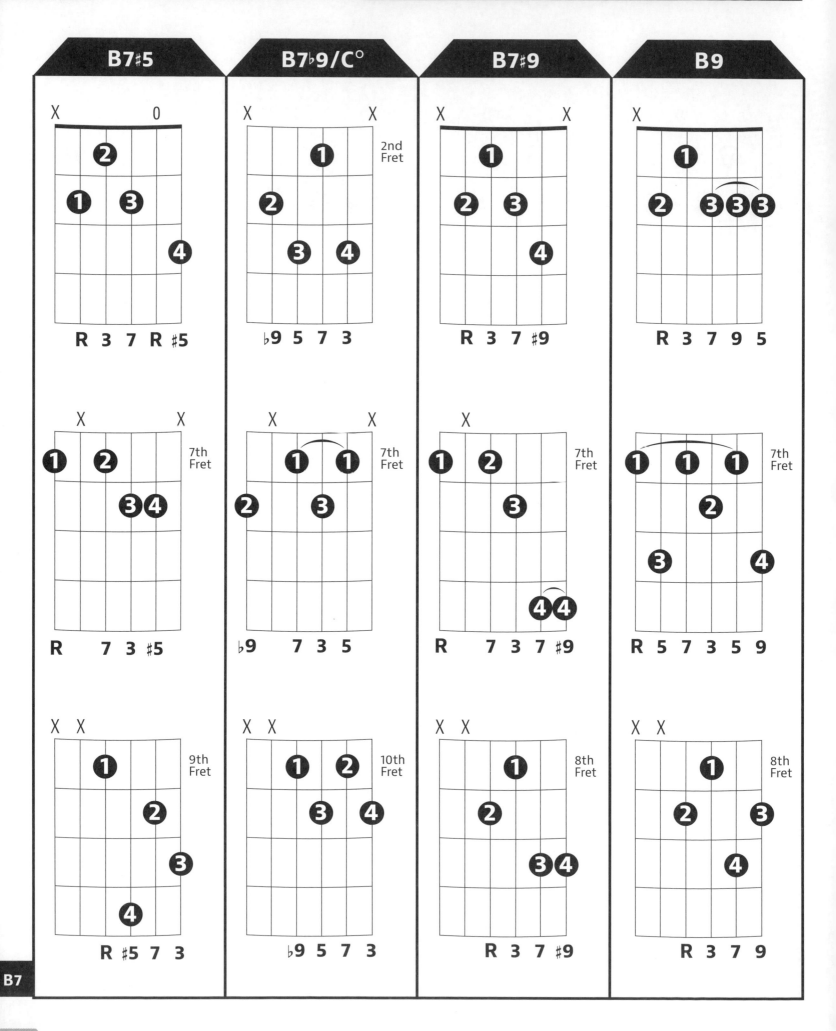

B7#5

X   0

R 3 7 R #5

X   X   7th Fret

R   7 3 #5

X X   9th Fret

R #5 7 3

B7♭9/C°

X   X   2nd Fret

♭9 5 7 3

X   X   7th Fret

♭9   7 3 5

X X   10th Fret

♭9 5 7 3

B7#9

X   X

R 3 7 #9

X   7th Fret

R   7 3 7 #9

X X   8th Fret

R 3 7 #9

B9

X

R 3 7 9 5

7th Fret

R 5 7 3 5 9

X X   8th Fret

R 3 7 9

B7

Seventh   B

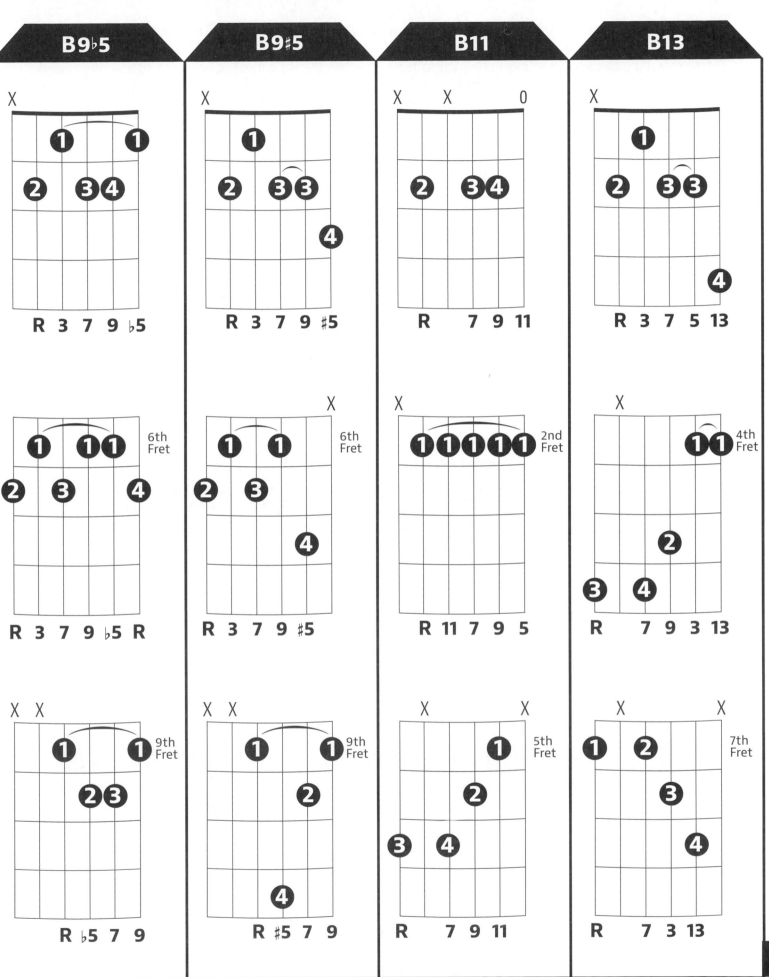

Modes

Modes, while derived from major scales, are harmonically quite distinct. The rules of substitution and alteration continue to apply, although chords will take on new harmonic functions in each mode. On these two pages, you will find diatonic triads (with one seventh chord) for each of the seven modes (major is called the Ionian mode in the Greek modal system). You will also find a few defining chord progressions for each mode. A defining progression is one which cannot exist in any other mode.

Each mode has its own unique sequence of half steps and whole steps which helps identify it. For example, the half step between i and II in the Phrygian mode is as unique and important as the harmonic functions of the i and II chords themselves.

Ionian Mode (Major)		
Scale Degree	Type of Triad	Defining Progressions
I	Major	I - IV - V7
ii	Minor	V7 - I
iii	Minor	ii - V7 - I
IV	Major	
V7	Seventh	
vi	Minor	
vii°	Diminished	
Sequence of Half Steps and Whole Steps: whole - whole - half - whole - whole - whole - half		

Dorian Mode		
Scale Degree	Type of Triad	Defining Progressions
i	Minor	i - ii
ii	Minor	i - IV7
III	Major	
IV7	Seventh	
v	Minor	
vi°	Diminished	
VII	Major	
Sequence of Half Steps and Whole Steps: whole - half - whole - whole - whole - half - whole		

Phrygian Mode		
Scale Degree	Type of Triad	Defining Progressions
i	Minor	i - II
II	Major	
III7	Seventh	
iv	Minor	
v°	Diminished	
VI	Major	
vii	Minor	
Sequence of Half Steps and Whole Steps: half - whole - whole - whole - half - whole - whole		

Lydian Mode

Scale Degree	Type of Triad	Defining Progressions
I	Major	I – II7
II7	Seventh	
iii	Minor	
iv°	Diminished	
V	Major	
vi	Minor	
vii	Minor	

Sequence of Half Steps and Whole Steps: whole - whole - whole - half - whole - whole - half

Mixolydian Mode

Scale Degree	Type of Triad	Defining Progressions
I7	Seventh	VII – I7
ii	Minor	vi – VII – I7
iii°	Diminished	
IV	Major	
v	Minor	
vi	Minor	
VII	Major	

Sequence of Half Steps and Whole Steps: whole - whole - half - whole - whole - half - whole

Aeolian Mode (Natural Minor)

Scale Degree	Type of Triad	Defining Progressions
i	Minor	i – iv- v
ii°	Diminished	VI – VII7 – i
III	Major	
iv	Minor	
v	Minor	
VI	Major	
VII7	Seventh	

Sequence of Half Steps and Whole Steps: whole - half - whole - whole - half - whole - whole

Locrian Mode

Scale Degree	Type of Triad	Defining Progressions
i°	Diminished	i°
II	Major	
iii	Minor	
iv	Minor	
V	Major	
VI7	Seventh	
vii	Minor	

Sequence of Half Steps and Whole Steps: half - whole - whole - half - whole - whole - whole

Blues

Blues progressions are unique in that they contain more than one dominant seventh chord (although generally only the V7 chord is heard to retain its dominant function). A standard blues progression will often contain the following chords: I7, IV7, and V7. As previously discussed, the notes making up the V7 chord can be found in the major scale of the root chord's key; the I7 and IV7, however, contain notes that do not naturally occur in the scale.

The table below shows the blues scale as it relates to the major scale, and the way the steps of the scale may be interpreted in relation to each of the three main chords in a blues progression (I7, IV7, and V7).

As you can see, each note of the scale may be seen as part of a standard substitute or altered chord. Therefore, you can play every note of a blues scale over every chord in a simple blues progression (something that cannot be done in major or modal keys).

Scale Step (compared to Major)	In I7	In IV7	In V7
1	Root	5	sus4
♭3	♭3	♭7	♯5
4	sus4	Root	♭7
♭5	♭5	♭3	♯9
5	5	9	Root
♭7	♭7	4	♭3